Classic Quilts

LEISURE ARTS, INC. • Maumelle, Arkansas

ISBN-13/EAN: 978-1-4647-4329-0
UPC: 0-28906-06652-4

table of contents

{ These vintage and vintage-style quilts are true classics from every corner of quilt-making history. }

And classic patterns can help you make wonderful new quilts!

That's because all quilts spring from the same desire to make something beautiful and useful. Follow our patterns to recreate these quilts "as is," or remake them to suit your taste. We think you'll agree this collection of table toppers, wall hangings, and bed quilts can be your foundation—your building blocks—for a houseful of quilted treasures. After all, what makes a quilt yours is how you make it—with your choice of fabric and colors, and your individual flair!

trip around the world

If you want to make a quilt with plenty of color, consider a design that uses the simplest piecing. The entire Trip Around the World quilt top is considered a one-patch block because it doesn't repeat. Instead, it uses same-size squares arranged in a concentric color pattern.

FINISHED QUILT SIZE:
$78^{3}/_{4}$" x $78^{3}/_{4}$" (200 cm x 200 cm)

YARDAGE REQUIREMENTS

Yardage is based on 43"/44" (109 cm/112 cm) wide fabric.

2 3/8 yds (2.2 m) of green print fabric for outer borders
2 1/4 yds (2.1 m) of yellow print fabric for middle borders
2 1/8 yds (1.9 m) of red print fabric for inner borders
1/2 yd (46 cm) **each** of medium yellow, light yellow, navy, dark blue, medium blue, light blue, red, dark pink, medium pink, light pink, olive green, dark green, medium green, light green, orange, and dark yellow print fabrics
7 1/4 yds (6.6 m) of fabric for backing
1 yd (91 cm) of fabric for binding
86" x 86" (218 cm x 218 cm) square of batting

CUTTING THE PIECES

*Follow **Rotary Cutting**, page 39, to cut fabric. Cut all strips across the selvage-to-selvage width of the fabric unless otherwise indicated. Borders include extra length for "insurance" and will be trimmed after assembling quilt top center. All measurements include 1/4" seam allowances.*

From green print fabric:

- Cut 2 *lengthwise* **side outer borders** 3" x 77 1/4".
- Cut 2 *lengthwise* **top/bottom outer borders** 3" x 82 1/4".

From yellow print fabric:

- Cut 2 *lengthwise* **side middle borders** 2 1/2" x 73 1/4".
- Cut 2 *lengthwise* **top/bottom middle borders** 2 1/2" x 77 1/4".

From red print fabric:

- Cut 2 *lengthwise* **side inner borders** 2 1/2" x 69 1/4".
- Cut 2 *lengthwise* **top/bottom inner borders** 2 1/2" x 73 1/4".

From dark blue, medium blue, light blue, red, dark pink, medium pink, light pink, olive green, dark green, medium green, and light green print fabrics:

- Cut 6 **strips** 2 1/4"w from **each** fabric.

From orange, dark yellow, medium yellow, light yellow, and navy print fabrics:

- Cut 7 **strips** 2 1/4"w from **each** fabric.
  - From 1 navy strip and 1 dark yellow strip, cut 4 **squares** 2 1/4" x 2 1/4".
  - From 1 medium yellow strip and 1 light yellow strip, cut 8 **squares** 2 1/4" x 2 1/4".
  - From 1 orange strip, cut 1 **center square** 2 1/4" x 2 1/4".

ASSEMBLING THE QUILT TOP

*Follow **Piecing**, page 39, and **Pressing**, page 40, to assemble the quilt top.*

1. Sew strips together in color order shown to make **Strip Set 1**. Make 6 **Strip Set 1's**.

2. With right sides together and matching long raw edges, sew final lengthwise seam of **Strip Set 1** to form a tube (**Fig. 1**). Repeat with remaining Strip Set 1's.

Strip Set 1
(make 6)

Fig. 1

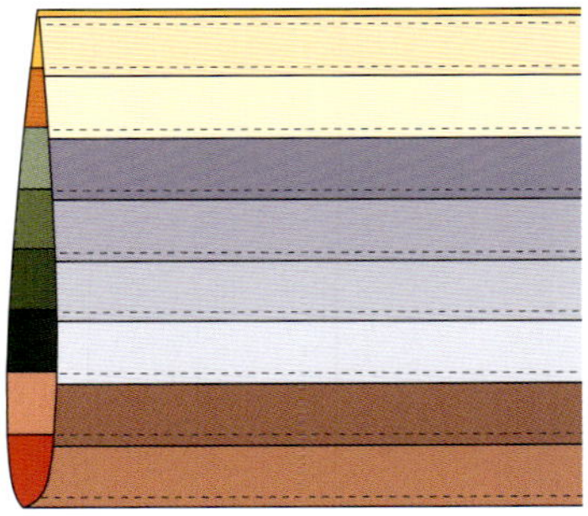

3. Referring to **Fig. 2**, cut across Strip Sets at $2^1/_4$" intervals to make 84 circular **Strip Units**.

4. Referring to **Section** diagrams, working from top to bottom, and laying strips horizontally on a flat surface, determine where to remove stitching from **Strip Unit** (**Fig. 3**). Carefully arrange and sew **Strip Units** in correct order to make **Section A**. Make 2 **Section A's**.

5. In same manner, arrange and sew **Strip Units** in correct order to make **Section B**. Make 2 **Section B's**.

Fig. 2

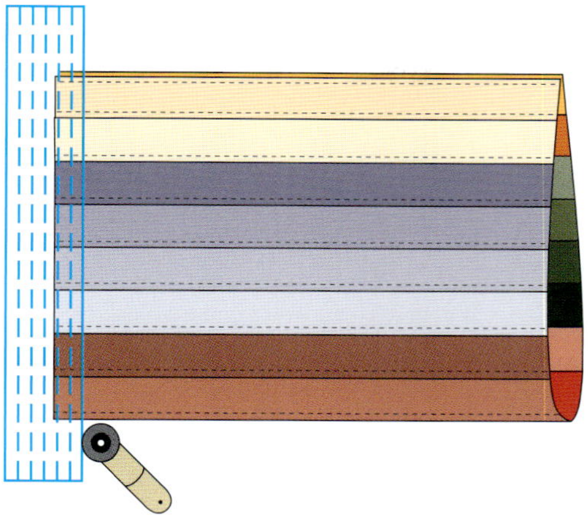

Strip Unit
(make 84)

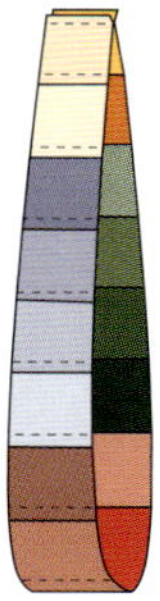

Fig. 3

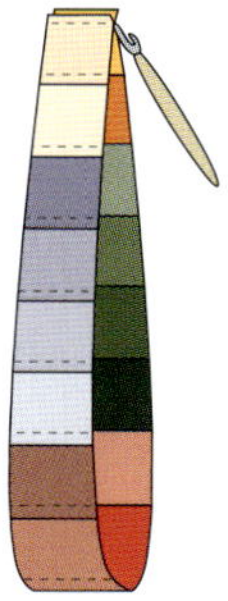

Section A
(make 2)

Section B
(make 2)

6. Laying strips vertically, carefully remove seam and arrange and sew **Strip Units** in correct order to make **Section C**. Make 2 **Section C's**. Arrange and sew **Strip Units** in correct order to make **Section D**. Make 2 **Section D's**.

7. Sew 1 medium yellow, 2 light yellow, and 1 navy **square** together to make each **Section E**. Make 4 **Section E's**.

8. Use a seam ripper to remove seam between medium yellow and dark yellow squares of one **Strip Unit**. To make **Section F**, sew 1 dark yellow **square** to 1 end of **Strip Unit**. Sew 1 medium yellow **square** to opposite end of **Strip Unit**. Make 4 **Section F's**.

9. Refer to **Assembly Diagram** to sew **Sections** together to make quilt top center.

10. Follow **Adding Squared Borders**, page 40, to add **side**, then **top** and **bottom inner borders** to center section. Repeat to add **middle** and **outer borders** to complete **Quilt Top**.

Section C
(make 2)

Section D
(make 2)

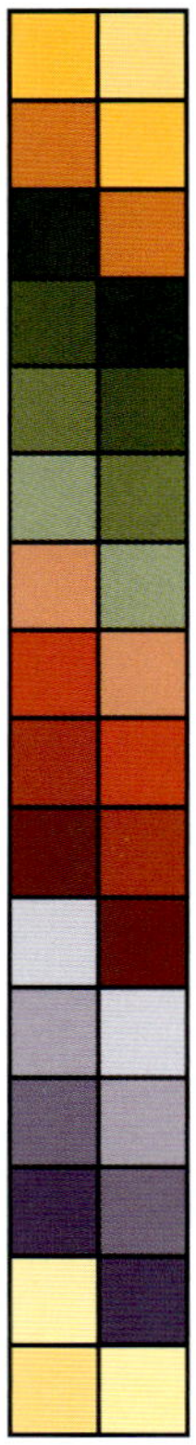

Section E
(make 4)

Section F
(make 4)

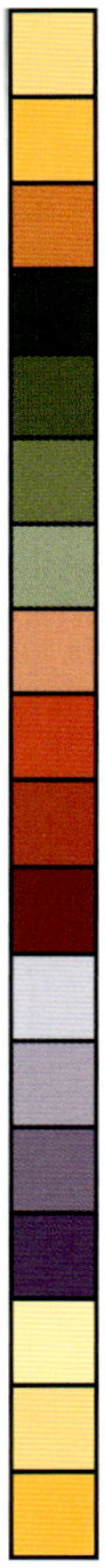

COMPLETING THE QUILT

1. Follow **Quilting**, page 41, to mark, layer, and quilt. Our quilt is hand quilted in diagonal lines across the pieced-square section and in the ditch along each border.

2. Cut a 30" square of binding fabric. Follow **Binding**, page 44, to bind quilt using 2 1/2"w continuous bias binding with overlapped corners.

Assembly Diagram

tree of life

The Bible is a source of many American quilt block names, and these blocks can vary widely, with entirely different patterns sharing the same name. This is true of Tree of Life blocks. Most are pieced "on point." They can have two, three, four, or more rows of "leaves." The blocks in this particular quilt are unusual because a small strip of red fabric rather than a solid triangle indicates the ground beneath the tree.

FINISHED BLOCK SIZE:
9¹/₄" x 9¹/₄"" (23 cm x 23 cm)

FINISHED QUILT SIZE:
69" x 86" (175 cm x 218 cm)

*We simplified the piecing of this quilt by substituting solid setting triangles for the half blocks used on the edges of our antique quilt (see **Assembly Diagram**, page 14). We also resized the too-small quilt to fit a traditional twin-size bed.*

YARDAGE REQUIREMENTS

Yardage is based on 43"/44" (109 cm/112 cm) wide fabric.

$4\frac{3}{8}$ yds (4 m) of red solid fabric
$2\frac{1}{4}$ yds (2.1 m) of cream solid fabric
2 yds (1.8 m) of green solid fabric
$5\frac{1}{4}$ yds (4.8 m) of fabric for backing
1 yd (91 cm) of fabric for binding
77" x 94" (196 cm x 239 cm) square of batting

CUTTING THE PIECES

*Follow **Rotary Cutting**, page 39, to cut fabric. Cut all strips across the selvage-to-selvage width of the fabric unless otherwise indicated. Borders include extra length for "insurance" and will be trimmed after assembling quilt top center. All measurements include $\frac{1}{4}$" seam allowances.*

From red solid fabric:

- Cut 2 strips $14\frac{3}{8}$"w. From these strips, cut 4 squares $14\frac{3}{8}$" x $14\frac{3}{8}$". Cut squares twice diagonally to make 16 **setting triangles** (you will need 14 and have 2 left over).
- Cut 3 strips $3\frac{1}{4}$"w. From these strips, cut 31 **sashing squares** $3\frac{1}{4}$" x $3\frac{1}{4}$".
- Cut 16 strips $1\frac{1}{2}$"w. From these strips, cut 32 **short borders** $1\frac{1}{2}$" x $8\frac{3}{4}$" and 32 **long borders** $1\frac{1}{2}$" x $9\frac{3}{4}$".
- Cut 4 strips $1\frac{1}{2}$"w. From these strips, cut 32 **trunks** $1\frac{1}{2}$" x $4\frac{1}{2}$".
- Cut 1 strip $5\frac{1}{8}$"w. From this strip, cut 5 squares $5\frac{1}{8}$" x $5\frac{1}{8}$". Cut squares twice diagonally to make 20 **sashing triangles** (you will need 18 and have 2 left over).
- Cut 3 strips $6\frac{3}{8}$"w. From these strips, cut 16 squares $6\frac{3}{8}$" x $6\frac{3}{8}$". Cut squares once diagonally to make 32 **large triangles**.
- Cut 2 strips 2"w. From these strips, cut 32 **large squares** 2" x 2".
- Cut 18 strips $2\frac{3}{8}$"w. From these strips, cut 288 **very large squares** $2\frac{3}{8}$" x $2\frac{3}{8}$" for triangle-squares.
- Cut 2 squares $7\frac{1}{2}$" x $7\frac{1}{2}$". Cut squares once diagonally to make 4 **corner setting triangles**.

From cream solid fabric:

- Cut 4 strips $1\frac{7}{8}$"w. From these strips, cut 64 **medium squares** $1\frac{7}{8}$" x $1\frac{7}{8}$".
- Cut 1 strip $1\frac{1}{4}$"w. From these strip, cut 32 **small squares** $1\frac{1}{4}$" x $1\frac{1}{4}$".
- Cut 3 strips 6"w. From these strips, cut 16 squares 6" x 6". Cut squares twice diagonally to make 64 **small triangles**.
- Cut 18 strips $2\frac{3}{8}$"w. From these strips, cut 288 **very large squares** $2\frac{3}{8}$" x $2\frac{3}{8}$" for triangle-squares.

From green solid fabric:

- Cut 20 strips $3\frac{1}{4}$"w. From these strips, cut 80 **sashing strips** $3\frac{1}{4}$" x $9\frac{3}{4}$".

ASSEMBLING THE QUILT TOP

*Follow **Piecing**, page 39, and **Pressing**, page 40, to assemble the quilt top.*

1. Draw a diagonal line on wrong side of each cream **very large square**. With right sides together place 1 cream very large square on top of 1 red **very large square**. Stitch seam $\frac{1}{4}$" from each side of drawn line (**Fig. 1**).
2. Cut along drawn line and press seam allowances to darker fabric to make 2 **Triangle-Squares**. Make 576 **Triangle-Squares**. Trim each Triangle-Square to $1\frac{7}{8}$" x $1\frac{7}{8}$".

Fig. 1

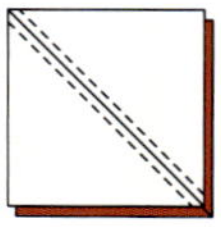

Triangle-Square
(make 576)

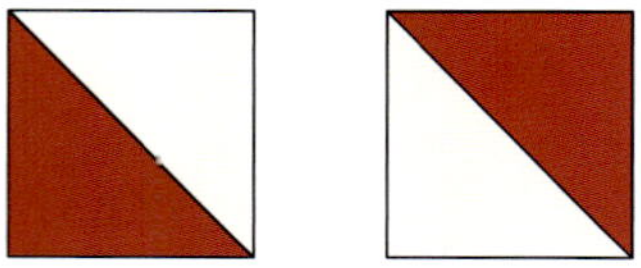

3. Sew 10 **triangle-squares** and 2 **medium squares** together to make **Unit 1**. Make 32 **Unit 1's**.
4. Sew 8 **triangle-squares** together to make **Unit 2**. Make 32 **Unit 2's**.
5. Sew 1 **large triangle**, 1 **Unit 2**, and 1 **Unit 1** together to make **Unit 3**. Make 32 **Unit 3's**.
6. Referring to **Fig. 2a** and **2b**, sew 1 **trunk** and 2 **small triangles** together. Trim trunk even with triangles to make **Unit 4**. Make 32 **Unit 4's**.
7. Matching right sides and raw edges, place 1 **small square** and 1 **large square** together. Sew diagonally across **small square** (**Fig. 3a**). Trim 1/4" beyond stitching (**Fig. 3b**) and press open to make **Unit 5**. Make 32 **Unit 5's**.
8. Matching right sides and raw edges, place 1 **Unit 5** and 1 **Unit 4** together. Sew diagonally across **Unit 5** (**Fig. 4a**). Trim 1/4" beyond stitching (**Fig. 4b**) and press open to make **Unit 6**. Make 32 **Unit 6's**.

Unit 1
(make 32)

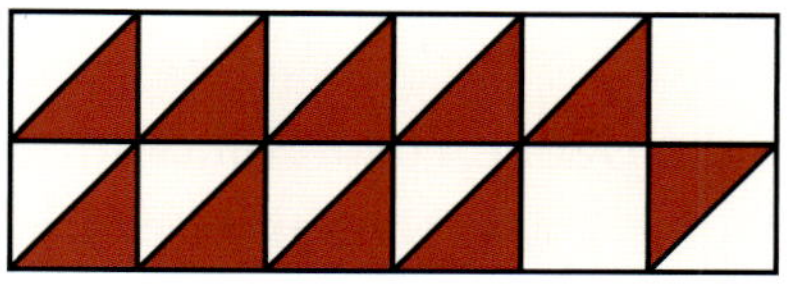

Fig. 2a

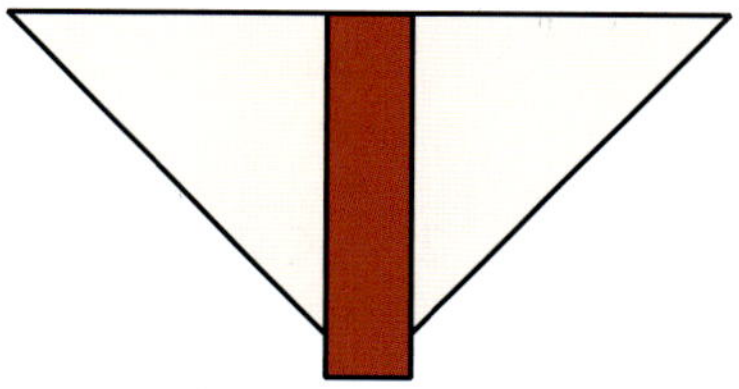

Fig. 3a

Fig. 4a

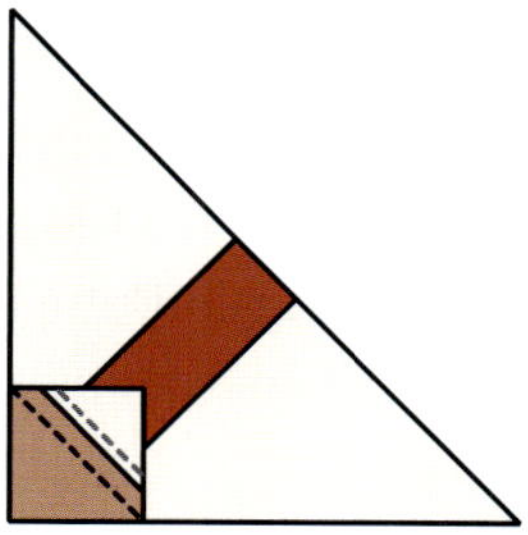

Unit 2
(make 32)

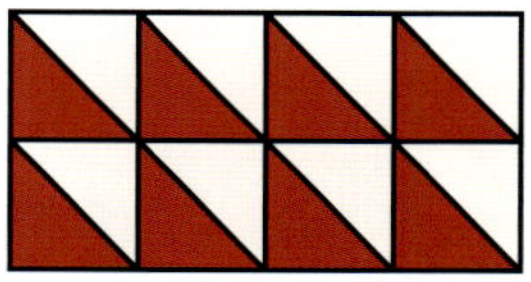

Fig. 2b

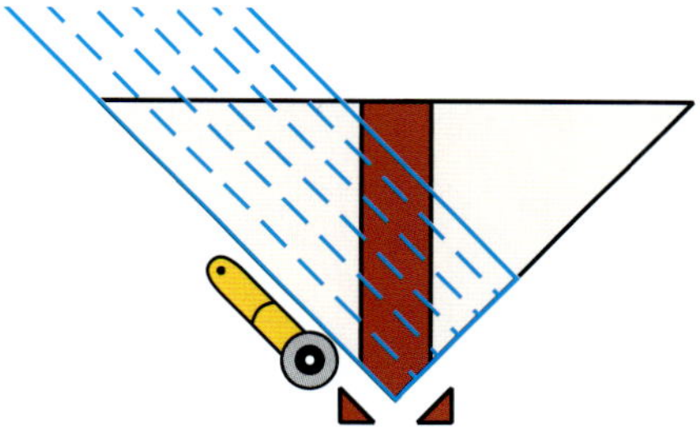

Fig. 3b

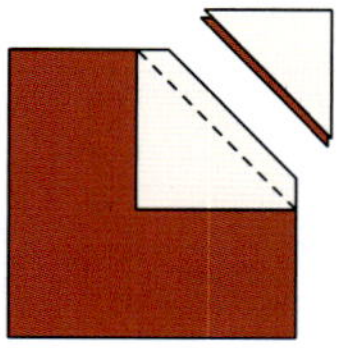

Fig. 4b

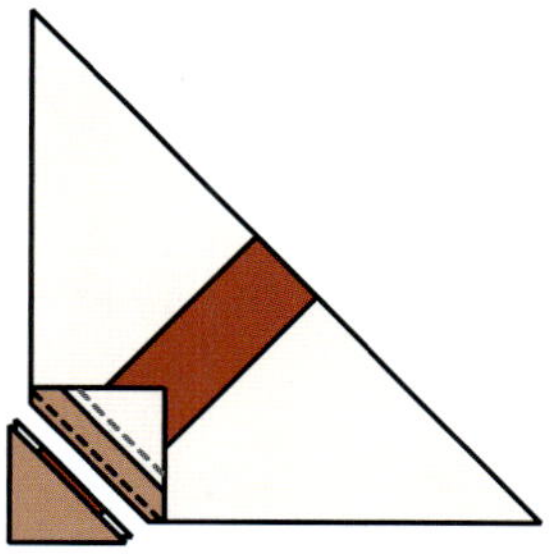

Unit 3
(make 32)

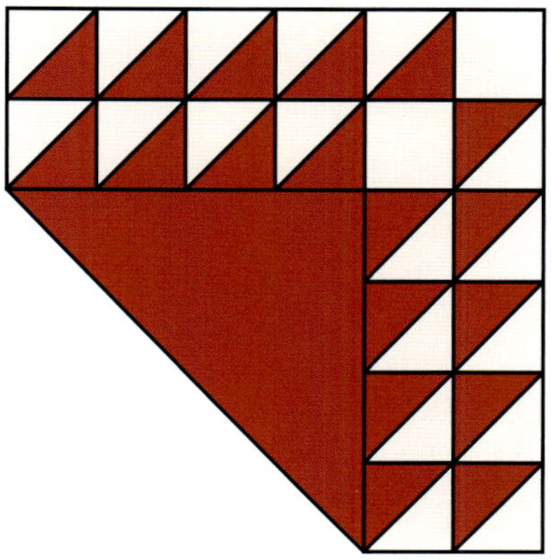

Unit 4
(make 32)

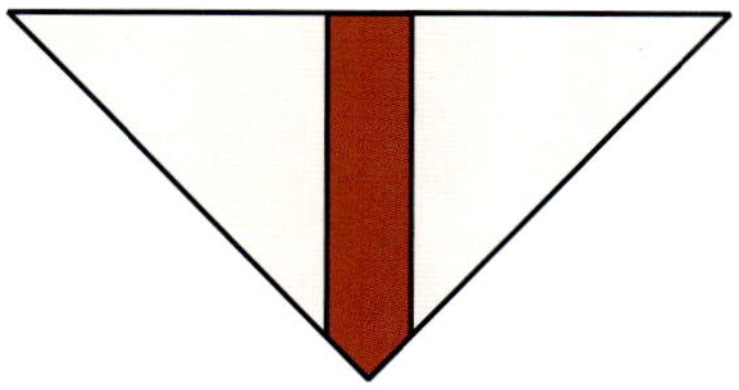

Unit 5
(make 32)

Unit 6
(make 32)

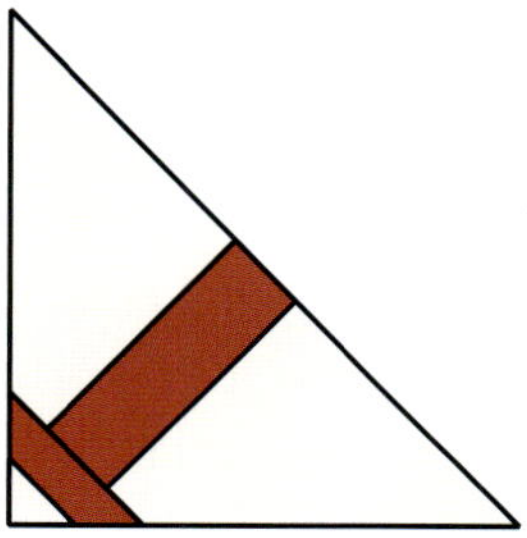

9. Sew 1 **Unit 3** and 1 **Unit 6** together to make **Unit 7**. Make 32 **Unit 7's**.
10. Sew **short**, then **long borders** to **Unit 7** to complete **Block**. Make 32 **Blocks**.
11. Referring to **Assembly Diagram**, sew **corner setting triangles**, **sashing triangles**, **sashing strips**, **setting triangles**, **sashing squares**, and **Blocks** together into **Rows**. Sew **Rows** together to complete **Quilt Top**.

Unit 7
(make 32)

Block
(make 32)

COMPLETING THE QUILT TOP

1. Follow **Quilting**, page 41, to mark, layer, and quilt using **Quilting Diagram** as a suggestion. Our quilt is hand quilted.
2. Cut a 31" square of binding fabric. Follow **Binding**, page 44, to bind quilt using $2^1/_2$"w continuous bias binding with mitered corners.

Quilting Diagram

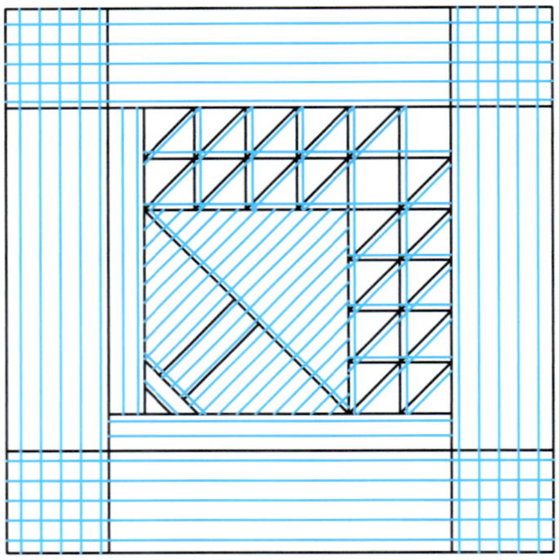

Assembly Diagram

Quilt Top Diagram

hourglasses and geese

This crisp blue-and-white quilt combines the simple four-triangle Hourglass block with Flying Geese sashing. These two designs are some of the most common components of quilt making. The Hourglass block is also called Bowtie or X block. If you begin looking for it, you will see it as a smaller unit in other popular blocks, such as Ohio Star or Crosses-and-Losses. Getting perfect points on the Flying Geese is easy with the stitch-and-flip technique. It also speeds the process of creating this refreshing quilt top.

FINISHED BLOCK SIZE:
8¹/₄" x 8¹/₄" (21 cm x 21 cm)

FINISHED QUILT SIZE:
80³/₄" x 91³/₄" (205 cm x 233 cm)

MARGARET E. MURIE
blink

YARDAGE REQUIREMENTS

Yardage is based on 43"/44" (109 cm/112 cm) wide fabric.

$6^{3}/_{4}$ yds (6.2 m) of cream print fabric
$6^{1}/_{4}$ yds (5.7 m) of blue solid fabric
$7^{1}/_{2}$ yds (6.9 m) of fabric for backing
1 yd (91 cm) of fabric for binding
89" x 100" (226 cm x 254 cm) rectangle of batting

CUTTING THE PIECES

*Follow **Rotary Cutting**, page 39, to cut fabric. Cut all strips across the selvage-to-selvage width of the fabric. All measurements include $^{1}/_{4}$" seam allowances.*

From cream print fabric:

- Cut 7 strips $9^{5}/_{8}$"w. From these strips, cut 28 **large squares** $9^{5}/_{8}$" x $9^{5}/_{8}$".
- Cut 87 strips $1^{7}/_{8}$"w. From these strips, cut 1812 **small squares** $1^{7}/_{8}$" x $1^{7}/_{8}$".

From blue solid fabric:

- Cut 7 strips $9^{5}/_{8}$"w. From these strips, cut 28 **large squares** $9^{5}/_{8}$" x $9^{5}/_{8}$".
- Cut 44 strips $3^{1}/_{4}$"w. From these strips, cut 906 **rectangles** $1^{7}/_{8}$" x $3^{1}/_{4}$".

ASSEMBLING THE QUILT TOP

*Follow **Piecing**, page 39, and **Pressing**, page 40, to assemble the quilt top.*

1. Draw a diagonal line on wrong side of each cream print **large square**. With right sides together place 1 cream print large square on top of 1 blue solid **large square**. Stitch seam $^{1}/_{4}$" from each side of drawn line (**Fig. 1**).
2. Cut along drawn line and press seam allowances to darker fabric to make 2 **Triangle-Squares**. Make 56 **Triangle-Squares**.
3. Referring to **Fig. 2**, place 2 **triangle-squares** right sides and opposite colors together, matching seams. Referring to **Fig. 3**, draw a diagonal line. Stitch $^{1}/_{4}$" from each side of line. Cut apart on drawn line and press open to make 2 **Blocks**. Repeat with remaining **triangle-squares** to make a total of 56 **Blocks**. Trim each Block to $8^{3}/_{4}$" x $8^{3}/_{4}$".
4. Place 1 **small square** on 1 **rectangle** and stitch diagonally as shown in **Fig. 4**. Trim $^{1}/_{4}$" from stitching line as shown in **Fig. 5**. Press open, pressing seam allowance toward darker fabric.
5. Place 1 **small square** on opposite end of **rectangle**. Stitch diagonally as shown in **Fig. 6**. Trim $^{1}/_{4}$" from stitching line as shown in **Fig. 7**. Press open, pressing seam allowance toward darker fabric to make **Unit 1**.
6. Repeat Steps 4 and 5 using remaining **small squares** and **rectangles** to make a total of 906 **Unit 1's**.
7. Sew 6 **Unit 1's** together to make **Sashing Unit**. Make 127 **Sashing Units**.

Fig. 1

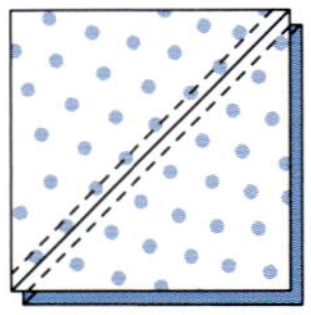

Triangle-Square
(make 56)

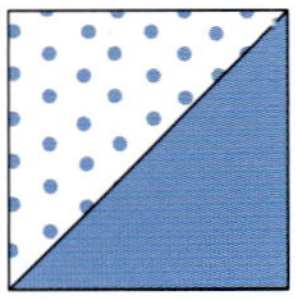

Fig. 2

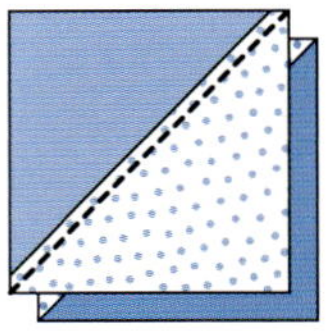

Fig. 3

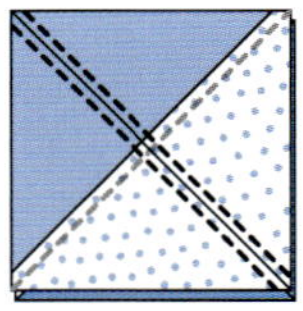

Block
(make 56)

Fig. 4

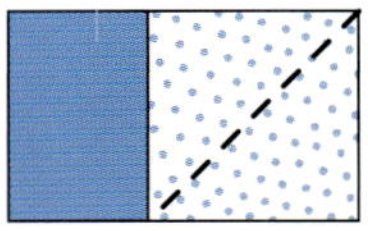

Fig. 5

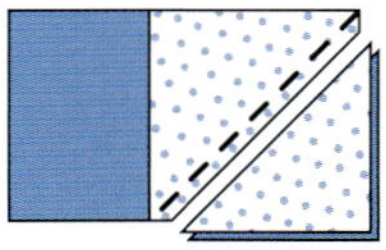

Fig. 6

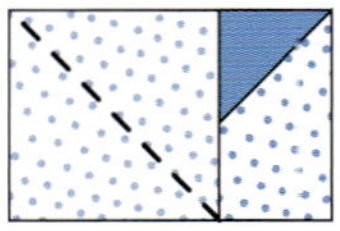

Fig. 7

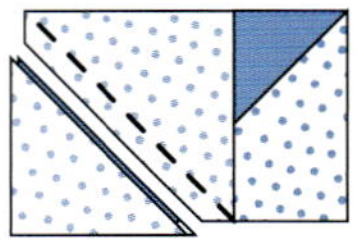

Unit 1
(make 906)

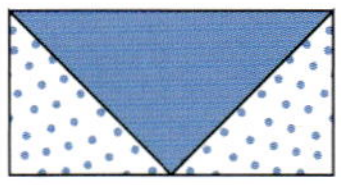

Sashing Unit
(make 127)

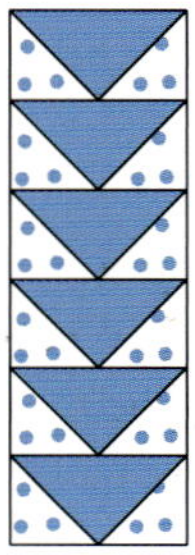

Sashing Square
(make 72)

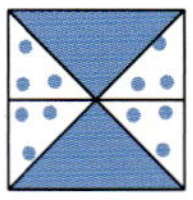

8. Sew 2 **Unit 1's** together to make **Sashing Square**. Make 72 **Sashing Squares**.
9. Sew 8 **Sashing Squares** and 7 **Sashing Units** together to make **Sashing Row**. Make 9 **Sashing Rows**.
10. Sew 8 **Sashing Units** and 7 **Blocks** together to make **Row**. Make 8 **Rows**.
11. Referring to **Quilt Top Diagram**, sew **Sashing Rows** and **Rows** together to complete **Quilt Top**.

Sashing Row
(make 9)

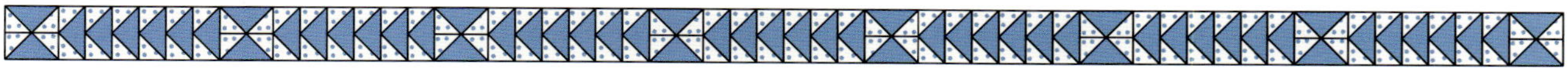

Row
(make 8)

COMPLETING THE QUILT TOP

1. Follow **Quilting**, page 41, to mark, layer, and quilt using **Quilting Diagram** as a suggestion. Our quilt is hand quilted.
2. Cut a 32" square of binding fabric. Follow **Binding**, page 44, to bind quilt using $2^1/_2$"w continuous bias binding with mitered corners.

Quilting Diagram

Quilt Top Diagram

rail fence

It's hard to imagine an easier block to sew than Rail Fence. You just sew seven long strips side-by-side, then cut the large pieced unit into equal blocks. When choosing colors for your quilt, have fun. Pick the hues that appeal to you. The maker of this quilt used the print fabrics of the late nineteenth century.

FINISHED BLOCK SIZE:
8³/₄" x 8³/₄" (22 cm x 22 cm)

FINISHED QUILT SIZE:
76¹/₄" x 76¹/₄" (194 cm x 194 cm)

YARDAGE REQUIREMENTS

Yardage is based on 43"/44" (109 cm/112 cm) wide fabric.

$1^{1}/_{2}$ yds (1.4 m) **total** of assorted dark print fabrics
$1^{1}/_{2}$ yds (1.4 m) **total** of assorted light print fabrics
$2^{1}/_{8}$ yds (1.9 m) **total** of assorted medium print fabrics
2 yds (1.8 m) of blue solid fabric
$2^{1}/_{4}$ yds (2.1 m) of pink print fabric
$7^{1}/_{8}$ yds (6.5 m) of fabric for backing
1 yd (91 cm) of fabric for binding
85" x 85" (216 cm x 216 cm) square of batting

CUTTING THE PIECES

*Follow **Rotary Cutting**, page 39, to cut fabric. Cut all strips across the selvage-to-selvage width of the fabric unless otherwise indicated. Borders include extra length for "insurance" and will be trimmed after assembling quilt top center. All measurements include $^{1}/_{4}$" seam allowances.*

From assorted dark print fabrics:

- Cut 26 **strips** $1^{3}/_{4}$" wide.

From assorted light print fabrics:

- Cut 26 **strips** $1^{3}/_{4}$" wide.

From assorted medium print fabrics:

- Cut 39 **strips** $1^{3}/_{4}$" wide.

From blue solid fabric:

- Cut 2 *lengthwise* **top** and **bottom inner borders** $1^{3}/_{4}$" x $65^{3}/_{4}$".
- Cut 2 *lengthwise* **side inner borders** $1^{3}/_{4}$" x $68^{1}/_{4}$".

From pink print fabric:

- Cut 2 *lengthwise* **top** and **bottom outer borders** $6^{1}/_{4}$" x $68^{1}/_{4}$".
- Cut 2 *lengthwise* **side outer borders** $6^{1}/_{4}$" x $79^{3}/_{4}$".

ASSEMBLING THE QUILT TOP

*Follow **Piecing**, page 39, and **Pressing**, page 40, to assemble the quilt top.*

1. Referring to **Strip Set Diagram**, sew 2 **dark**, 2 **light**, and 3 **medium strips** together to make 1 **Strip Set**. Make 13 **Strip Sets**.

2. Cut across Strip Sets at $9^{1}/_{4}$" intervals to make **Rail Fence Block**. Make 49 **Rail Fence Blocks**.

3. Referring to **Quilt Top Diagram** for orientation, sew 7 **Rail Fence Blocks** together to make **Row**. Make 7 **Rows**.

4. Sew Rows together to make quilt top center.

5. Follow **Adding Squared Borders**, page 40, to sew **top** and **bottom inner borders**, then **side inner borders** to center section. Repeat to add **outer borders** to center section to complete piecing the **Quilt Top**.

Strip Set
(make 13)

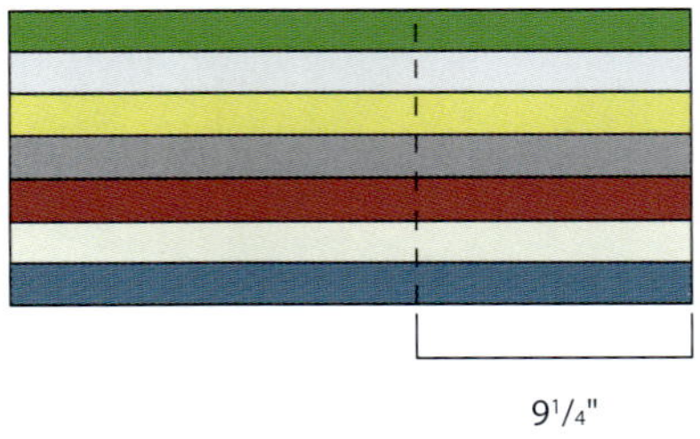

Rail Fence Block
(make 49)

COMPLETING THE QUILT TOP

1. Follow **Quilting**, page 41, to mark, layer, and quilt as desired. Our quilt is hand quilted with alternating parallel diagonal or vertical straight lines in the blocks. The borders are quilted with diagonal channel quilting.

2. Cut a 30" square of binding fabric. Follow **Binding**, page 44, to bind quilt using $2^1/_2$"w continuous bias binding with mitered corners.

Quilt Top Diagram

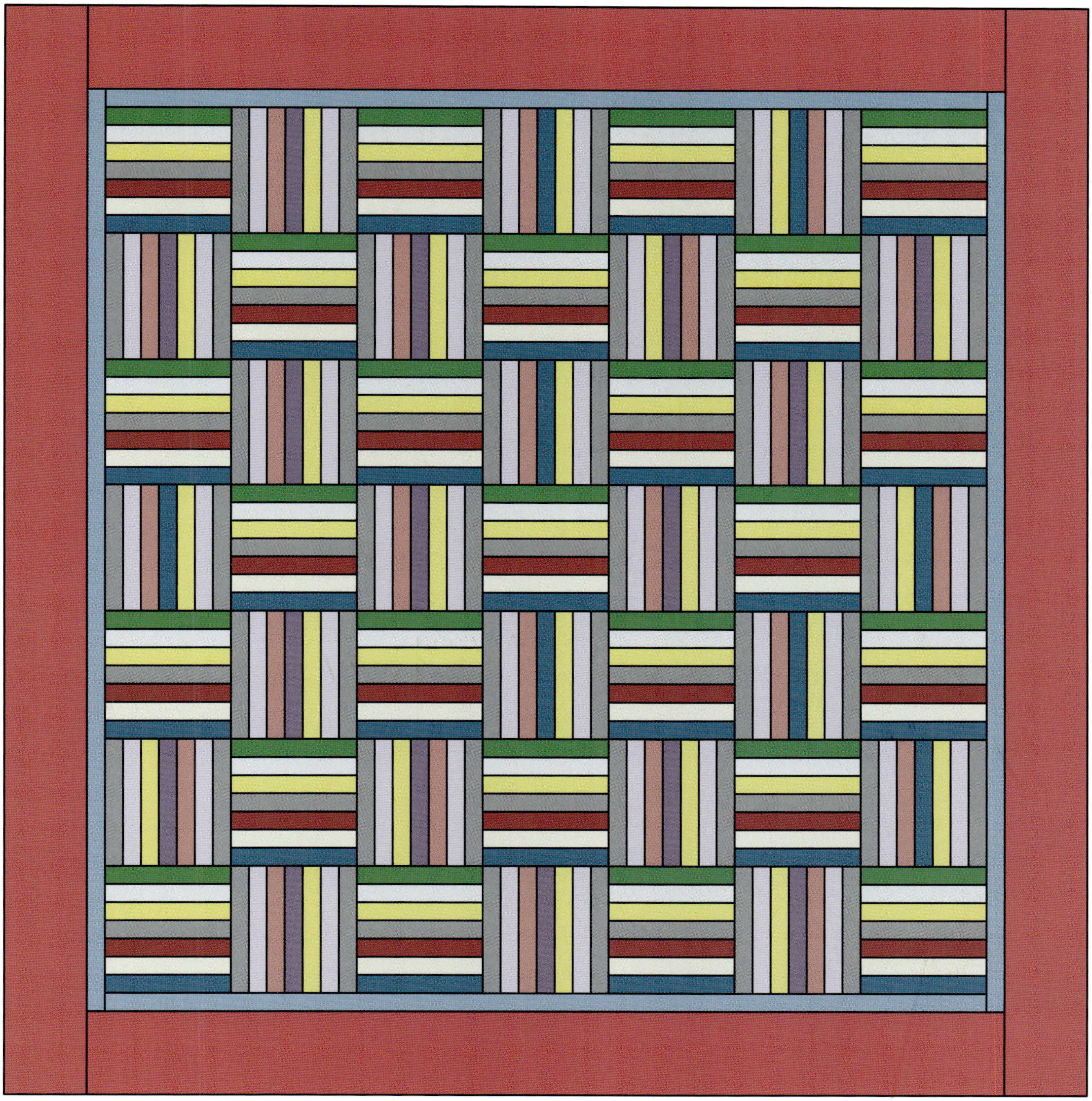

churn dash maze

The Churn Dash block has been appearing on quilts for more than 160 years. On some quilts, it's an equal nine-patch block, meaning its nine units are all the same size. In this Churn Dash Maze quilt, the block is an unequal nine patch with half-square triangles that are larger than the other pieces. The creator of this two-color quilt chose to set her blocks together with a fun sashing design called Garden Maze.

FINISHED BLOCK SIZE:
11¼" x 11¼" (29 cm x 29 cm)

FINISHED QUILT SIZE:
73½" x 90¼" (187 cm x 229 cm)

YARDAGE REQUIREMENTS

Yardage is based on 43"/44" (109 cm/112 cm) wide fabric.

$4\frac{1}{2}$ yds (4.1 m) of cream solid fabric
$4\frac{3}{4}$ yds (4.3 m) of navy print fabric
$6\frac{7}{8}$ yds (6.3 m) of fabric for backing
1 yd (91 cm) of fabric for binding
82" x 98" (208 cm x 249 cm) rectangle of batting

CUTTING THE PIECES

*Follow **Template Cutting** and **Rotary Cutting**, page 39, to cut fabric. Cut all strips across the selvage-to-selvage width of the fabric. All measurements include $\frac{1}{4}$" seam allowances.*

From cream solid fabric:

- Cut 6 strips $5\frac{1}{2}$"w. From these strips, cut 40 **squares** $5\frac{1}{2}$" x $5\frac{1}{2}$".
- Cut 4 strips $4\frac{3}{4}$"w. From these strips, cut 30 squares $4\frac{3}{4}$" x $4\frac{3}{4}$". Cut squares twice diagonally to make 120 **triangles**.
- Cut 17 **wide strips** 4"w.
- Cut 9 **strips** $2\frac{3}{4}$"w.

From navy print fabric:

- Cut 6 strips $5\frac{1}{2}$"w. From these strips, cut 40 **squares** $5\frac{1}{2}$" x $5\frac{1}{2}$".
- Cut 7 **strips** $2\frac{3}{4}$"w.
- Cut 34 **narrow strips** $1\frac{1}{2}$"w.
- Cut 60 **A's** using **Template A** pattern, page 28.
- Cut 30 **B's** using **Template B** pattern, page 28.

ASSEMBLING THE QUILT TOP

*Follow **Piecing**, page 39, and **Pressing**, page 40, to assemble the quilt top.*

1. Draw a diagonal line on wrong side of each cream solid **square**. With right sides together place 1 cream solid square on top of 1 navy print **square**. Stitch seam $\frac{1}{4}$" from each side of drawn line (**Fig. 1**).
2. Cut along drawn line and press seam allowances to darker fabric to make 2 **Triangle-Squares**. Make 80 **Triangle-Squares**. Trim each Triangle-Square to 5" x 5".
3. Sew 2 **strips** together to make **Strip Set A**. Make 3 Strip **Set A's**. Cut across **Strip Set A's** at $2\frac{3}{4}$" intervals to make 40 **Unit 1's**.
4. Sew 5 **strips** together to make **Strip Set B**. Make 2 **Strip Set B's**. Cut across **Strip Set B's** at $2\frac{3}{4}$" intervals to make 20 **Unit 2's**.

Fig. 1

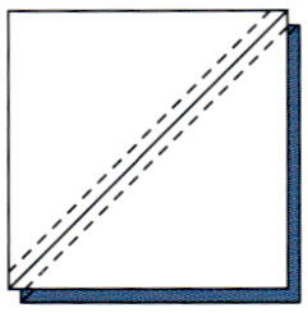

Triangle-Square
(make 80)

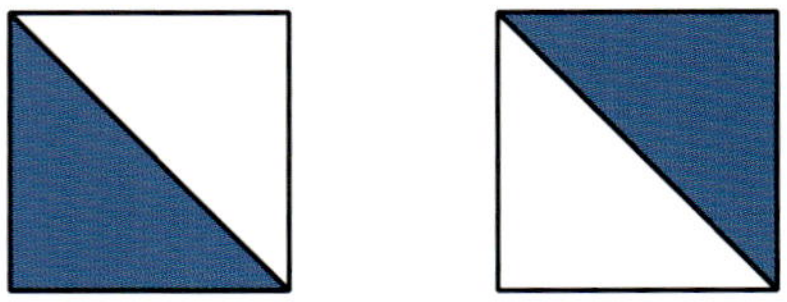

Strip Set A
(make 3)

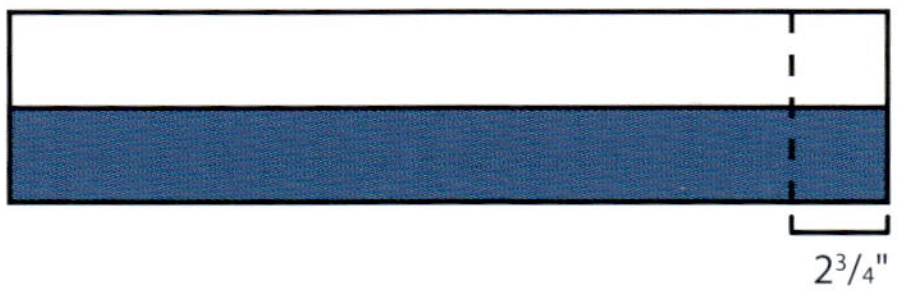

Unit 1
(make 40)

Strip Set B
(make 2)

Unit 2
(make 20)

5. Sew 2 **triangle-squares** and **1 Unit 1** together to make **Unit 3**. Make 40 **Unit 3's**.
6. Sew 2 **Unit 3's** and 1 **Unit 2** together to make **Block**. Make 20 **Blocks**.
7. Sew 1 **wide** and 2 **narrow strips** together to make **Strip Set C**. Make 17 **Strip Set C's**. Cut across **Strip Set C's** at 11$^{3}/_{4}$" intervals to make 49 **Sashing Units**.
8. Sew 2 **triangles** and 1 **A** together to make **Unit 4**. Make 60 **Unit 4's**.
9. Sew 2 **Unit 4's** and 1 **B** together to make **Sashing Square**. Make 30 **Sashing Squares**.
10. Sew 5 **Sashing Squares** and 4 **Sashing Units** together to make **Sashing Row**. Make 6 **Sashing Rows**.
11. Sew 5 **Sashing Units** and 4 **Blocks** together to make **Row**. Make 5 **Rows**.
12. Referring to **Quilt Top Diagram**, page 29, sew **Sashing Rows** and **Rows** together to complete **Quilt Top**.

Unit 3
(make 40)

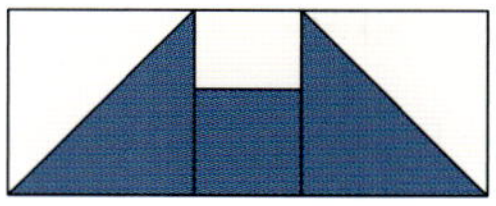

Block
(make 20)

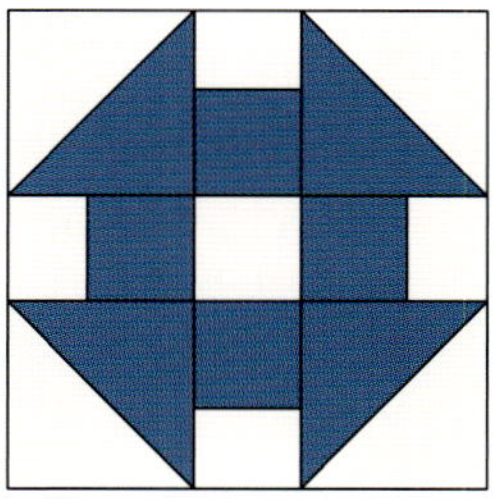

Strip Set C
(make 17)

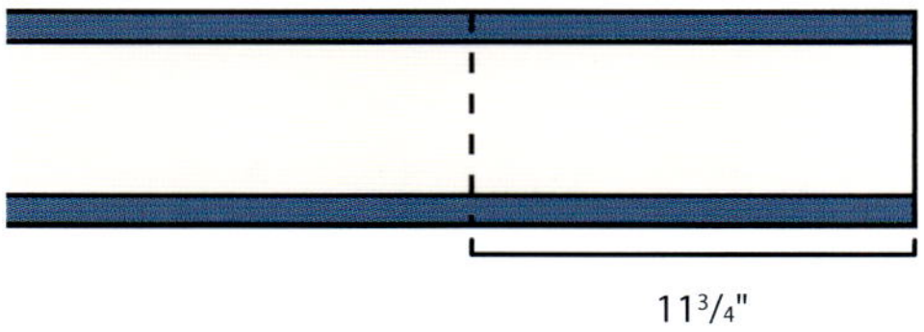

Sashing Unit
(make 49)

Unit 4
(make 60)

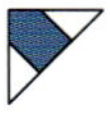

Sashing-Square
(make 30)

Sashing Row
(make 6)

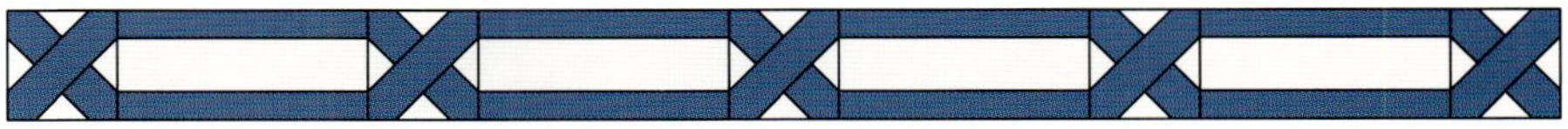

Row
(make 5)

COMPLETING THE QUILT TOP

1. Follow **Quilting**, page 41, to mark, layer, and quilt using **Quilting Diagram** as a suggestion. Our quilt is hand quilted.
2. Cut a 32" square of binding fabric. Follow **Binding**, page 44, to bind quilt using 2 1/2"w continuous bias binding with mitered corners.

Quilting Diagram

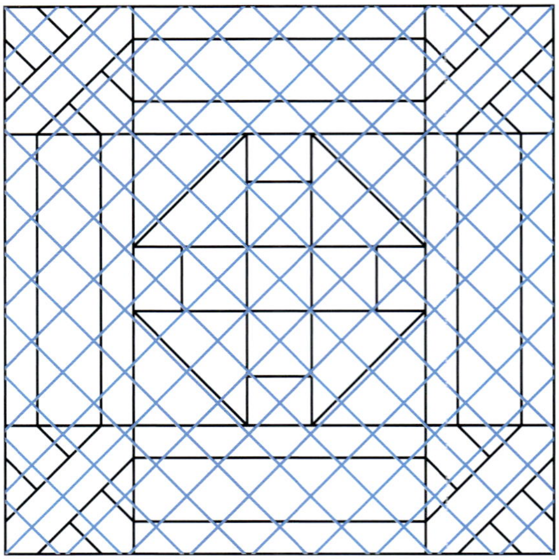

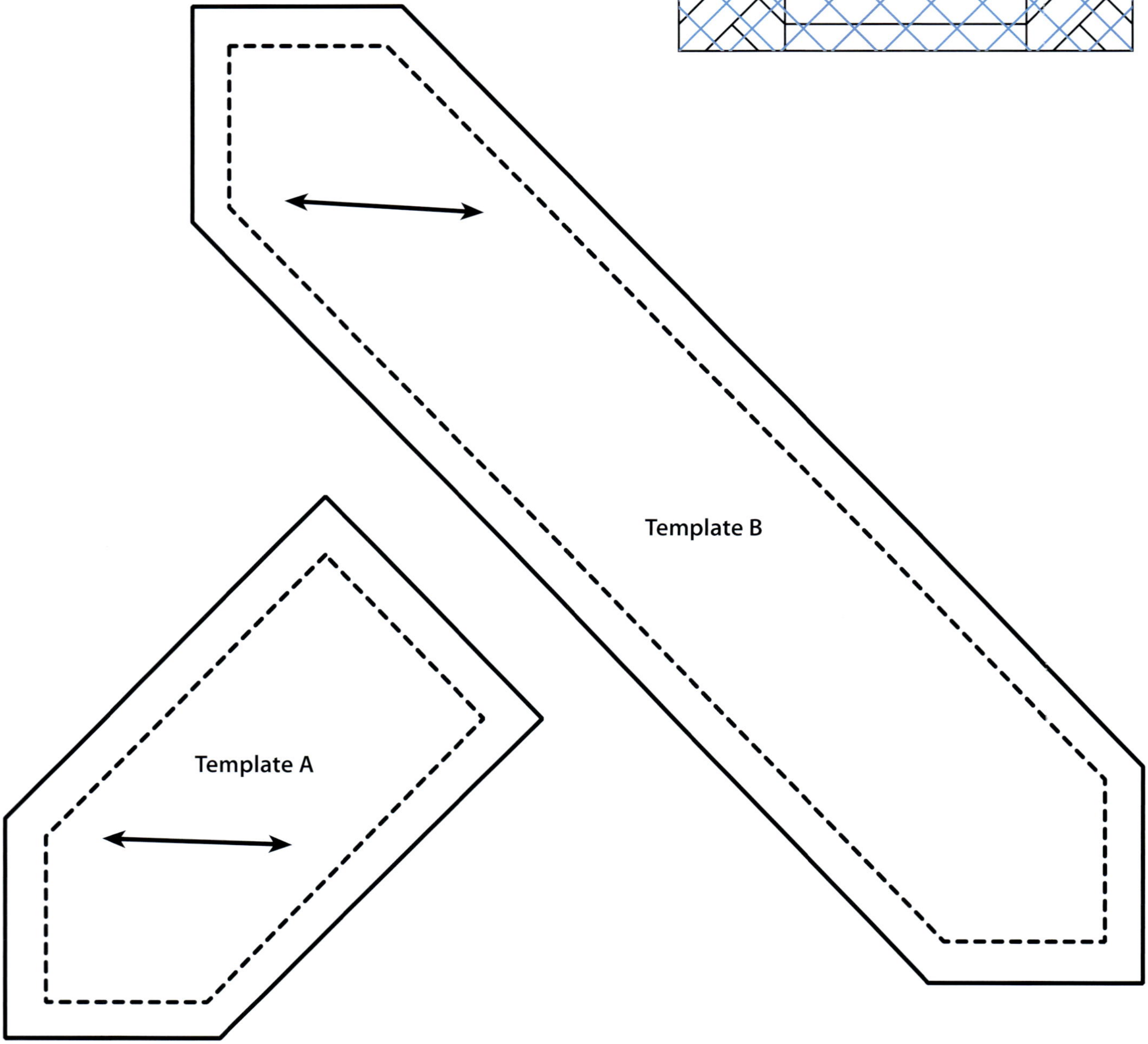

Quilt Top Diagram

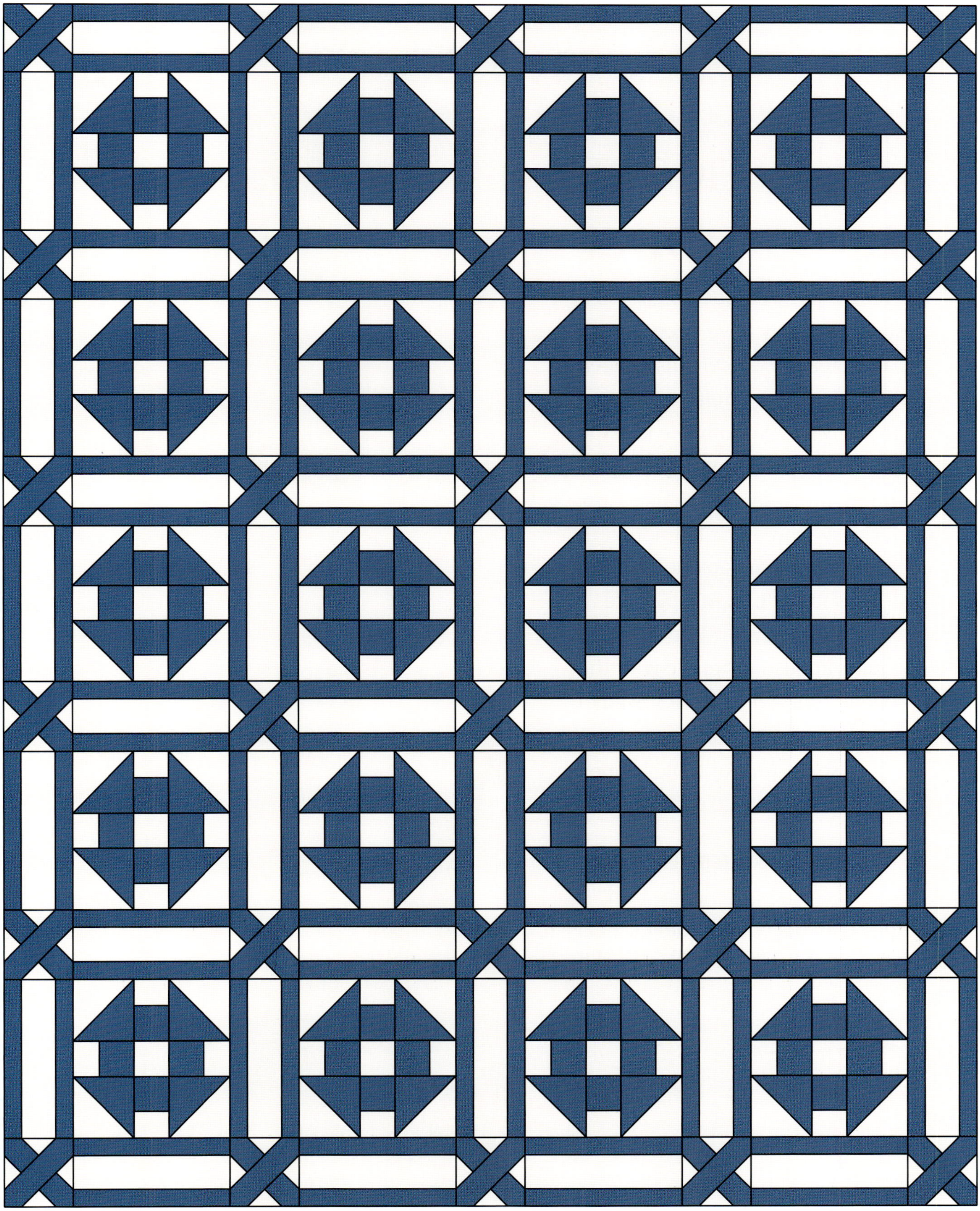

shoofly table topper

The blocks in this delectable Amish-style quilt may have been named for an American dessert that's been served in New England for more than 200 years. Shoofly pie is made using just a few simple ingredients, including molasses. For that reason, it's easy to imagine a nineteenth century Amish cook putting her fresh shoofly pies in a pie safe to keep the flies away. And since Amish quilts are usually made with the same solid-color fabrics used in Amish clothing, we chose solids for our table topper.

FINISHED BLOCK SIZE:
4⁷/₈" x 4⁷/₈" (12 cm x 12 cm)

FINISHED TABLE TOPPER SIZE:
35" x 42" (89 cm x 107 cm)

YARDAGE REQUIREMENTS

Yardage is based on 43"/44" (109 cm/112 cm) wide fabric.

1¼ yds (1.1 m) of black solid fabric
⅜ yd (34 cm) of dark red solid fabric
¼ yd (23 cm) of purple solid fabric
Scraps of assorted medium solids
Scraps of assorted dark solids
2¾ yds (2.5 m) of fabric for backing
¾ yd (69 cm) of fabric for binding
42" x 49" (107 cm x 124 cm) rectangle of batting

CUTTING THE PIECES

*Follow **Rotary Cutting**, page 39, to cut fabric. Cut all strips across the selvage-to-selvage width of the fabric. Borders include extra length for "insurance" and will be trimmed after assembling quilt top center. All measurements include ¼" seam allowances.*

From black solid fabric:

- Cut 2 **side outer borders** 5" x 36⅜".
- Cut 2 **top/bottom outer borders** 5" x 29½".
- Cut 1 strip 8¼"w. From this strip, cut 3 squares 8¼" x 8¼". Cut squares twice diagonally to make 12 **side triangles**. (You will need 10 and have 2 left over.)
- Cut 1 strip 5⅜"w. From this strip, cut 6 **setting squares** 5⅜" x 5⅜".
- Cut 1 strip 4⅜"w. From this strip, cut 2 squares 4⅜" x 4⅜". Cut squares once diagonally to make 4 **corner triangles**.

From dark red solid fabric:

- Cut 2 **side inner borders** 2⅝" x 36⅜".
- Cut 2 **top/bottom inner borders** 2⅝" x 25¼".

From purple solid fabric:

- Cut 4 **corner squares** 5" x 5".

From assorted medium solids:

- For **each** of 12 blocks, cut 2 **large squares** 2⅝" x 2⅝" for triangle-squares and 4 **small squares** 2⅛" x 2⅛".

From assorted dark solids:

- For **each** of 12 blocks, cut 2 **large squares** 2⅝" x 2⅝" for triangle-squares and 1 **small square** 2⅛" x 2⅛".

ASSEMBLING THE TOP

*Follow **Piecing**, page 39, and **Pressing**, page 40, to assemble the table topper.*

1. Draw a diagonal line on wrong side of each medium solid **large square**.
2. With right sides together place 1 medium solid large square on top of 1 dark solid **large square**. Stitch seam ¼" from each side of drawn line (**Fig. 1**).
3. Cut along drawn line and press seam allowances to darker fabric to make 2 **Triangle-Squares**. Make 4 **Triangle-Squares**. Trim each Triangle-Square to 2⅛" x 2⅛".
4. Sew 2 **triangle-squares** and 1 **small square** together to make **Unit 1**. Make 2 **Unit 1's**.
5. Sew 3 **small squares** together to make 1 **Unit 2**.
6. Sew **Unit 1's** and **Unit 2** together to make **Block**.
7. Repeat Steps 2-6 to make a total of 12 **Blocks**.
8. Referring to **Assembly Diagram**, sew **corner triangles**, **side triangles**, **Blocks**, and **setting squares** together into diagonal rows. Sew rows together to make center section of table topper.
9. Measure width across center of table topper. Trim top and bottom inner borders to determined measurement.

Fig. 1

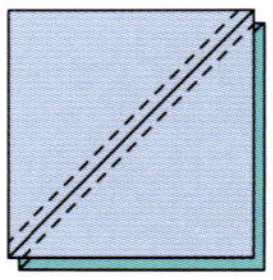

Triangle-Squares
(make 4)

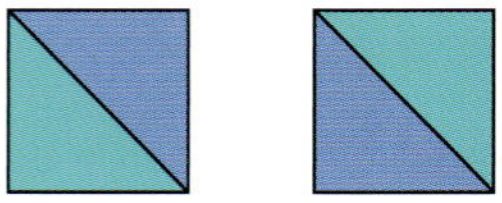

Unit 1
(make 2)

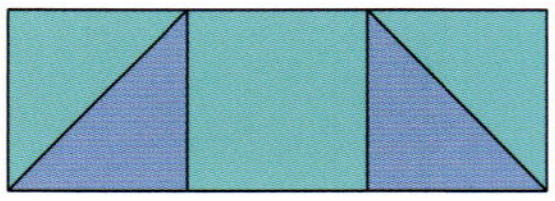

Unit 2
(make 1)

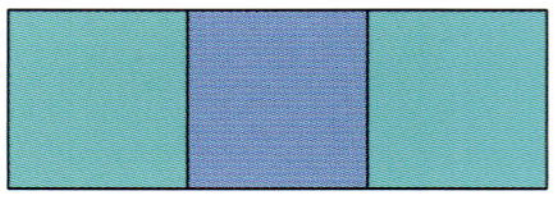

Block
(make 12)

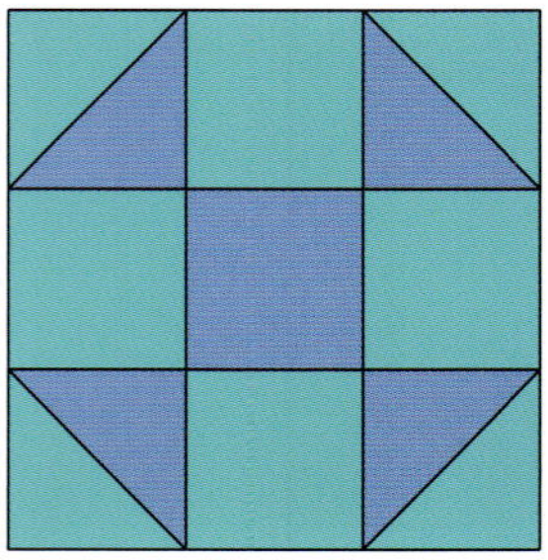

10. Sew **top** and **bottom inner borders** to center.
11. Measure length through center (including added borders). Trim side inner borders to determined measurement.
12. Sew side inner borders to table topper.
13. Measure width across center of table topper. Trim top and bottom outer borders to determined measurement. Measure length through center. Trim side outer borders to determined measurement.

Assembly Diagram

Quilting Diagram

14. Sew **top** and **bottom outer borders** to table topper. Sew 1 **corner square** to each end of **side outer borders**; sew on **borders** to complete **Table Topper**.

COMPLETING THE TABLE TOPPER

1. Follow **Quilting**, page 41, to mark, layer, and quilt using **Quilting Diagram** as a suggestion. Our table topper is hand quilted.
2. Cut a 22" square of binding fabric. Follow **Binding**, page 44, to bind table topper using $2^{1}/_{2}$"w continuous bias binding with overlapped corners.

Table Topper Top Diagram

log cabin wall hanging

The bold colors of this Amish-style wall hanging will add warmth to any surroundings. Log Cabin blocks are classic! They're perfect for beginning quilters and an excellent opportunity for anyone who likes to work with contrasting-color fabrics. With their half-dark/half-light appearance, Log Cabin blocks are a lot of fun to arrange into different patterns. This particular block setting is usually called "Barn Raising."

FINISHED BLOCK SIZE:
$5^3/_4$" x $5^3/_4$" (15 cm x 15 cm)

FINISHED WALL HANGING SIZE:
$38^1/_2$" x 50" (98 cm x 127 cm)

YARDAGE REQUIREMENTS

Yardage is based on 43"/44" (109 cm/112 cm) wide fabric.

- 2 yds (1.8 m) of black solid fabric
- 1 1/4 yds (1.1 m) of blue solid fabric
- 1/8 yd (11 cm) **each** of 24 assorted medium solids *(**Note:** Colors may be repeated for more than 1 Block.)*
- 3 1/4 yds (3 m) of fabric for backing
- 3/4 yd (69 cm) of fabric for binding
- 46 1/2" x 58" (118 cm x 147 cm) rectangle of batting

CUTTING THE PIECES

*Follow **Rotary Cutting**, page 39, to cut fabric. Cut all strips across the selvage-to-selvage width of the fabric unless otherwise indicated. Borders include extra length for "insurance" and will be trimmed after assembling quilt top center. All measurements include 1/4" seam allowances.*

From black solid fabric:

- Cut 18 **strips** 1 1/4"w.
- Cut 2 *lengthwise* **side outer borders** 5 1/2" x 43 1/2".
- Cut 2 *lengthwise* **top/bottom outer borders** 5 1/2" x 32".
- From remaining width, cut 3 strips 1 3/4"w. From these strips, cut 24 **squares** 1 3/4" x 1 3/4".

From blue solid fabric:

- Cut 2 *lengthwise* **side inner borders** 2 3/4" x 43 1/2".
- Cut 2 *lengthwise* **top/bottom inner borders** 2 3/4" x 27 1/2".
- From remaining width, cut 1 strip 5 1/2"w. From this strip, cut 4 **corner squares** 5 1/2" x 5 1/2".

From *each* of 24 assorted medium solids:

- Cut 1 **strip** 1 1/4"w.

ASSEMBLING THE WALL HANGING TOP

*Follow **Piecing**, page 39, and **Pressing**, page 40. Use a 1/4" seam allowance.*

1. Matching right sides and raw edges, place 1 medium solid **strip** and 1 black **square** together. Stitch as shown in **Fig. 1**. Trim strip even with square (**Fig. 2**); press open (**Fig. 3**).
2. Turn **square** 1/4 turn counter clockwise and repeat Step 1 to add the next "log" as shown in **Figs. 4-6**.
3. Repeat Step 2 to add black **strips** to remaining 2 sides of **square** (**Fig. 7**).

Fig. 1

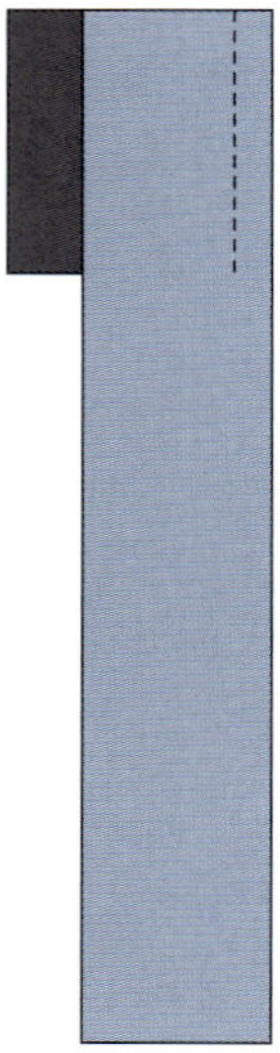

Fig. 2

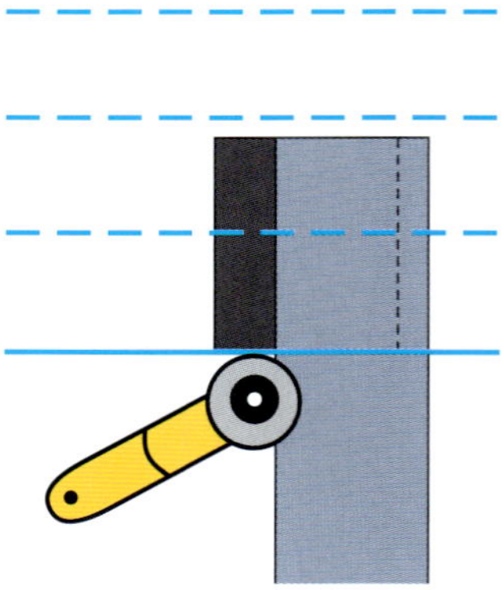

Fig. 3

Fig. 4

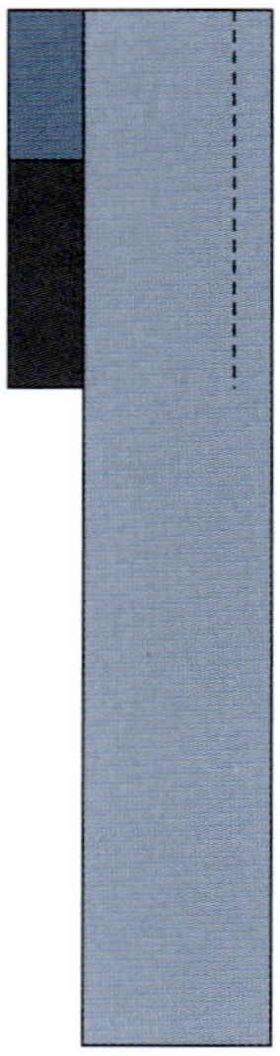

Fig.5

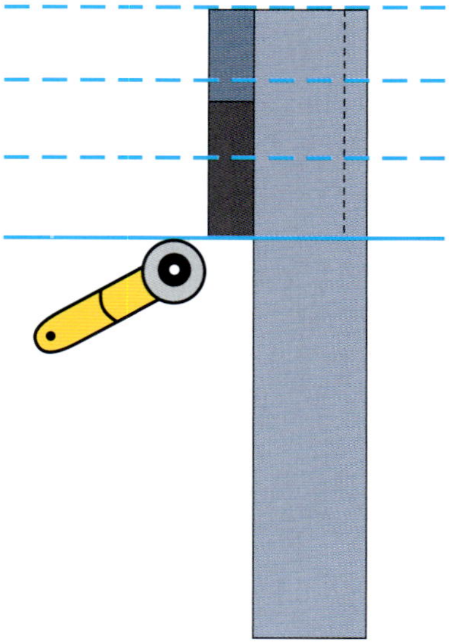

Fig. 6

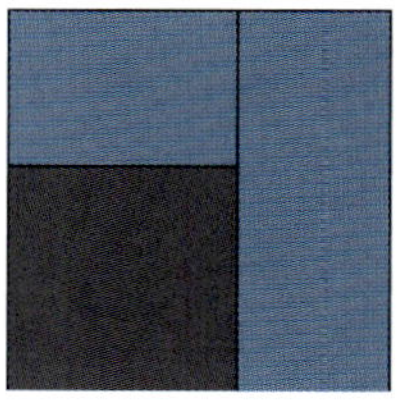

Fig. 7

4. Continue adding **strips**, alternating 2 medium solid strips and 2 black strips until there are 3 strips on each side of square to make **Block**.
5. Using remaining strips, repeat Steps 1-4 to make a total of 24 **Blocks**.
6. Referring to **Wall Hanging Top Diagram**, sew **Blocks** together into **Rows**. Sew **Rows** together to make center section of wall hanging top.
7. Follow **Adding Squared Borders**, page 40, to sew **top**, **bottom**, then **side inner borders** to center section.
8. Measure length of wall hanging top center across center of quilt. Trim side outer borders to determined length. Measure width of wall hanging center across center of quilt. Trim top/bottom outer borders to determined length.
9. Sew side outer borders to sides of wall hanging top center. Sew 1 corner square to each end of each top and bottom outer border. Sew top and bottom borders to wall hanging top.

Block
(make 24)

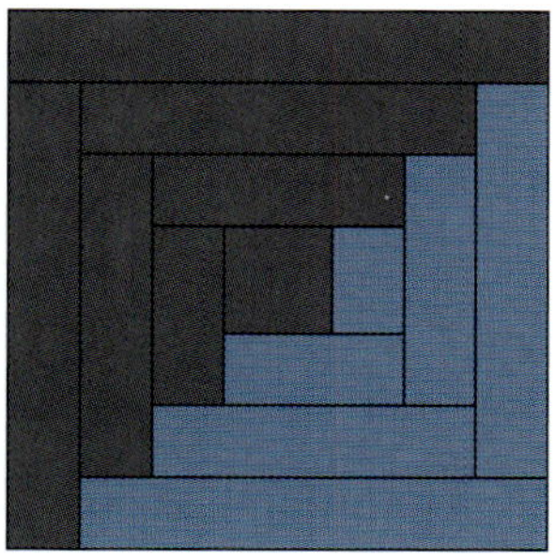

COMPLETING THE WALL HANGING

1. Follow **Quilting**, page 41, to mark, layer, and quilt, using **Quilting Diagram** as a suggestion. Our wall hanging is hand quilted.
2. Cut a 24" square of binding fabric. Follow **Binding**, page 44, to bind quilt using 2$^1/_2$"w continuous bias binding with overlapped corners.

Quilting Diagram

Wall Hanging Top Diagram

general instructions

To make your quilting easier and more enjoyable, we encourage you to carefully read all of the general instructions, study the color photographs, and familiarize yourself with the individual project instructions before beginning a project.

FABRICS

SELECTING FABRICS

Choose high-quality, medium-weight 100% cotton fabrics. All-cotton fabrics hold a crease better, fray less, and are easier to quilt than cotton/polyester blends.

Yardage requirements listed for each project are based on 43"/44" wide fabric with a "usable" width of 40" after shrinkage and trimming selvages. Actual usable width will probably vary slightly from fabric to fabric. Our recommended yardage lengths should be adequate for occasional re-squaring of fabric when many cuts are required.

PREPARING FABRICS

We recommend that all fabrics be washed, dried, and pressed before cutting. If fabrics are not pre-washed, washing the finished quilt will cause shrinkage and give it a more "antiqued" look and feel. Bright and dark colors, which may run, should always be washed before cutting. After washing and drying fabric, fold lengthwise with wrong sides together and matching selvages.

TEMPLATE CUTTING

Our piecing template patterns have 2 lines – a solid cutting line and a dashed line showing the 1/4" seam allowance.

1. To make a template from a pattern, use a permanent fine-point pen to carefully trace pattern onto template plastic, making sure to transfer all alignment and grainline markings. Cut out template along inner edge of drawn line. Check template against original pattern for accuracy.

2. To use a piecing template, place template on wrong side of fabric (unless otherwise indicated), aligning grainline on template with straight grain of fabric. Use a sharp fabric-marking pencil to draw around template. Transfer all alignment markings to fabric. Cut out fabric piece using scissors or rotary cutting equipment.

ROTARY CUTTING

Rotary cutting has brought speed and accuracy to quiltmaking by allowing quilters to easily cut strips of fabric and then cut those strips into smaller pieces.

- Place fabric on work surface with fold closest to you.
- Cut all strips from the selvage-to-selvage width of the fabric unless otherwise indicated in project instructions.
- Square left edge of fabric using rotary cutter and rulers (**Figs. 1 - 2**).

Fig. 1

Fig. 2

- To cut each strip required for a project, place ruler over cut edge of fabric, aligning desired marking on ruler with cut edge; make cut (**Fig. 3**).

Fig. 3

- When cutting several strips from a single piece of fabric, it is important to make sure that cuts remain at a perfect right angle to the fold; square fabric as needed.

PIECING

Precise cutting, followed by accurate piecing, will ensure that all pieces of quilt top fit together well.

- Set sewing machine stitch length for approximately 11 stitches per inch.
- Use neutral-colored general-purpose sewing thread (not quilting thread) in needle and in bobbin.
- An accurate $^{1}/_{4}$" seam allowance is *essential*. Presser feet that are $^{1}/_{4}$" wide are available for most sewing machines.
- When piecing, always place pieces right sides together and match raw edges; pin if necessary.
- Chain piecing saves time and will usually result in more accurate piecing.
- Trim away points of seam allowances that extend beyond edges of sewn pieces.

SEWING STRIP SETS

When there are several strips to assemble into a strip set, first sew strips together into pairs, then sew pairs together to form strip set. To help avoid distortion, sew seams in opposite directions (**Fig. 4**).

Fig. 4

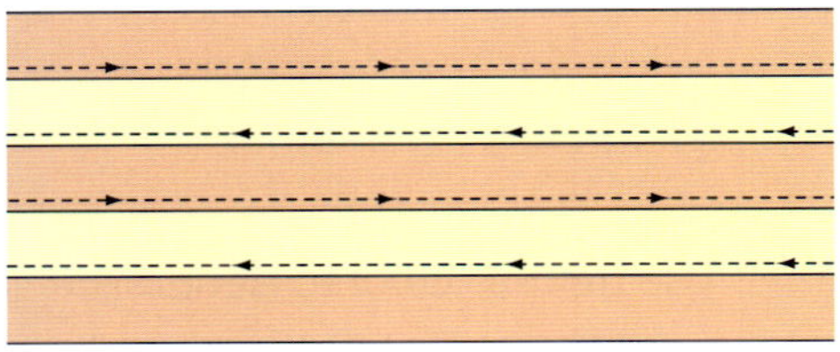

SEWING ACROSS SEAM INTERSECTIONS

When sewing across intersection of two seams, place pieces right sides together and match seams exactly, making sure seam allowances are pressed in opposite directions (**Fig. 5**).

Fig. 5

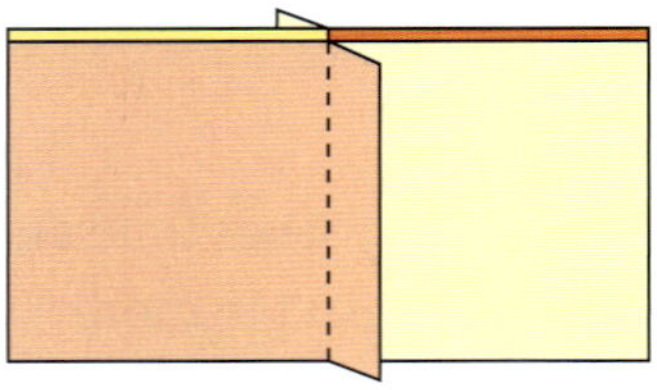

SEWING SHARP POINTS

To ensure sharp points when joining triangular or diagonal pieces, stitch across the center of the "X" (shown in pink) formed on wrong side by previous seams (**Fig. 6**).

Fig. 6

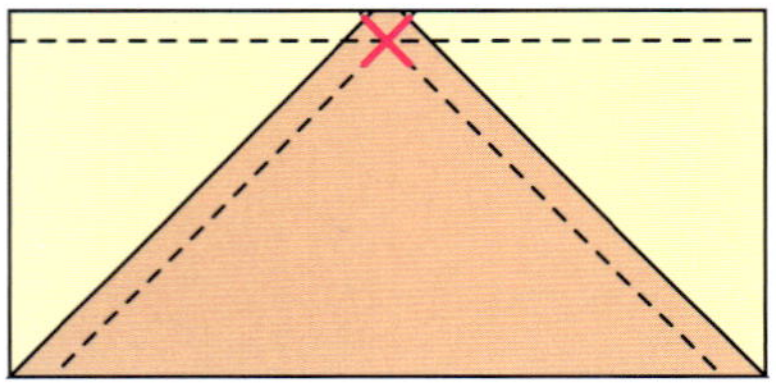

PRESSING

- Use steam iron set on "Cotton" for all pressing.
- Press after sewing each seam.
- Seam allowances are almost always pressed to one side, usually toward darker fabric. However, to reduce bulk it may occasionally be necessary to press seam allowances toward the lighter fabric or even to press them open.
- To prevent dark fabric seam allowance from showing through light fabric, trim darker seam allowance slightly narrower than lighter seam allowance.
- To press long seams, such as those in long strip sets, without curving or other distortion, lay strips across width of the ironing board.

BORDERS

Our instructions for cutting borders for bed-size quilts also include an extra 2" at each end for "insurance"; borders will be trimmed after measuring completed center section of quilt top. And, as always, you should match right sides and raw edges and use a ¼" seam allowance when sewing.

ADDING SQUARED BORDERS

1. Mark the center of each edge of quilt top (**Fig. 7**).

Fig. 7

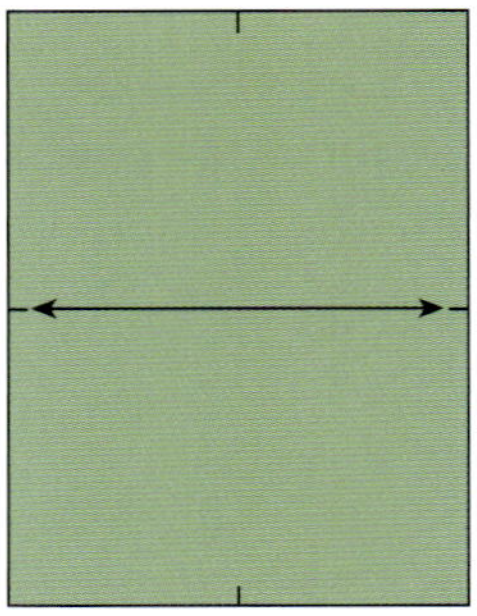

2. Squared borders are usually added to top and bottom, then side edges of the center section of a quilt top. To add top border, measure across center of quilt top to determine length of border (see **Fig. 10**). Trim border to the determined length.

3. Mark center of 1 long edge of border. Matching center marks and raw edges, pin border to quilt top; stitch.
4. Repeat Steps 2 and 3 to add bottom border to quilt top.
5. Measure center of quilt top (including attached borders) to determine length of side borders. Trim borders to the determined measurement. Repeat Step 3 to add side borders to quilt top (**Fig. 8**).

Fig. 8

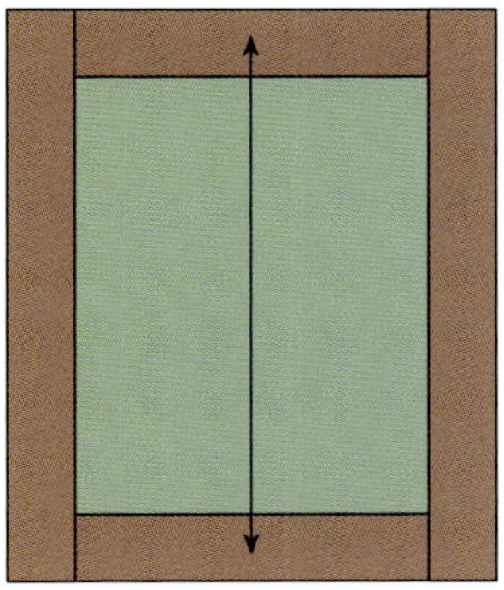

QUILTING

*Quilting holds the three layers (top, batting, and backing) of the quilt together and can be done by hand or machine. Because marking, layering, and quilting are interrelated and may be done in different orders depending on circumstances, please read entire **Quilting** section, pages 41 – 44, before beginning project.*

TYPES OF QUILTING DESIGNS

In the Ditch Quilting

Quilting along seamlines or along edges of appliquéd pieces is called "in the ditch" quilting. This type of quilting should be done on side **opposite** seam allowance and does not have to be marked.

Outline Quilting

Quilting a consistent distance, usually $^{1}/_{4}$", from seam or appliqué is called "outline" quilting. Outline quilting may be marked, or $^{1}/_{4}$" masking tape may be placed along seamlines for quilting guide. (Do not leave tape on quilt longer than necessary, since it may leave an adhesive residue.)

Motif Quilting

Quilting a design, such as a feathered wreath, is called "motif" quilting. This type of quilting should be marked before basting quilt layers together.

Echo Quilting

Quilting that follows the outline of an appliquéd or pieced design with two or more parallel lines is called "echo" quilting. This type of quilting does not need to be marked.

Channel Quilting

Quilting with straight, parallel lines is called "channel" quilting. This type of quilting may be marked or stitched using a guide.

Crosshatch Quilting

Quilting straight lines in a grid pattern is called "crosshatch" quilting. Lines may be stitched parallel to edges of quilt or stitched diagonally. This type of quilting may be marked or stitched using a guide.

Meandering Quilting

Quilting in random curved lines and swirls is called "meandering" quilting. Quilting lines should not cross or touch each other. This type of quilting does not need to be marked.

Stipple Quilting

Meandering quilting that is very closely spaced is called "stipple" quilting. Stippling will flatten the area quilted and is often stitched in background areas to raise appliquéd or pieced designs. This type of quilting does not need to be marked.

MARKING QUILTING LINES

Quilting lines may be marked using fabric marking pencils, chalk markers, water- or air-soluble pens, or lead pencils.

Simple quilting designs may be marked with chalk or chalk pencil after basting. A small area may be marked, then quilted, before moving to next area to be marked. Intricate designs should be marked before basting using a more durable marker.

Caution: Pressing may permanently set some marks. **Test** different markers **on scrap fabric** to find one that marks clearly and can be thoroughly removed.

A wide variety of pre-cut quilting stencils, as well as entire books of quilting patterns, are available. Using a stencil makes it easier to mark intricate or repetitive designs.

To make a stencil from a pattern, center template plastic over pattern and use a permanent marker to trace pattern onto plastic. Use a craft knife with single or double blade to cut channels along traced lines (**Fig. 9**).

Fig. 9

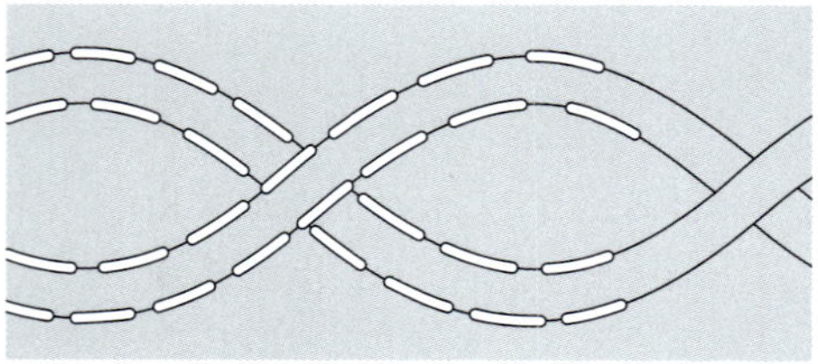

PREPARING THE BACKING

To allow for slight shifting of quilt top during quilting, backing should be approximately 4" larger on all sides. Yardage requirements listed for quilt backings are calculated for 43"/44"w fabric. Using 90"w or 108"w fabric for the backing of a bed-sized quilt may eliminate piecing. To piece a backing using 43"/44"w fabric, use the following instructions.

1. Measure length and width of quilt top; add 8" to each measurement.
2. If determined width is 79" or less, cut backing fabric into two lengths slightly longer than determined *length* measurement. Trim selvages. Place lengths with right sides facing and sew long edges together, forming tube (**Fig. 10**). Match seams and press along one fold (**Fig. 11**). Cut along pressed fold to form single piece (**Fig. 12**).

Fig. 10

Fig. 11

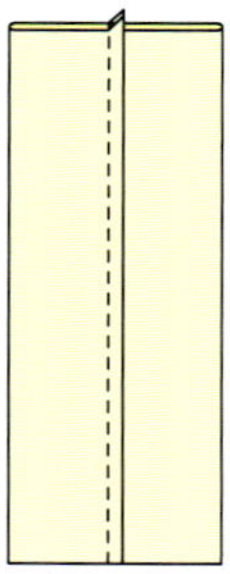

Fig. 12

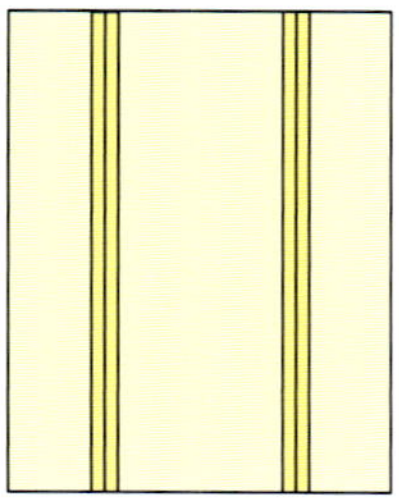

3. If determined width is more than 79", it may require less fabric yardage if the backing is pieced horizontally. Divide determined *length* measurement by 40" to determine how many widths will be needed. Cut required number of widths the determined *width* measurement. Trim selvages. Sew long edges together to form single piece.
4. Trim backing to size determined in Step 1; press seam allowances open.

CHOOSING THE BATTING

The appropriate batting will make quilting easier. For fine hand quilting, choose low-loft batting. All cotton or cotton/polyester blend battings work well for machine quilting because the cotton helps "grip" quilt layers. If quilt is to be tied, a high-loft batting, sometimes called extra-loft or fat batting, may be used to make quilt "fluffy."

Types of batting include cotton, polyester, wool, cotton/polyester blend, cotton/wool blend, and silk.

When selecting batting, refer to package labels for characteristics and care instructions. Cut batting same size as prepared backing.

ASSEMBLING THE QUILT

1. Examine wrong side of quilt top closely; trim any seam allowances and clip any threads that may show through front of the quilt. Press quilt top, being careful not to "set" any marked quilting lines.
2. Place backing *wrong* side up on flat surface. Use masking tape to tape edges of backing to surface. Place batting on top of backing fabric. Smooth batting gently, being careful not to stretch or tear. Center quilt top *right* side up on batting.
3. If hand quilting, begin in center and work toward outer edges to hand baste all layers together. Use long stitches and place basting lines approximately 4" apart (**Fig. 13**). Smooth fullness or wrinkles toward outer edges.

Fig. 13

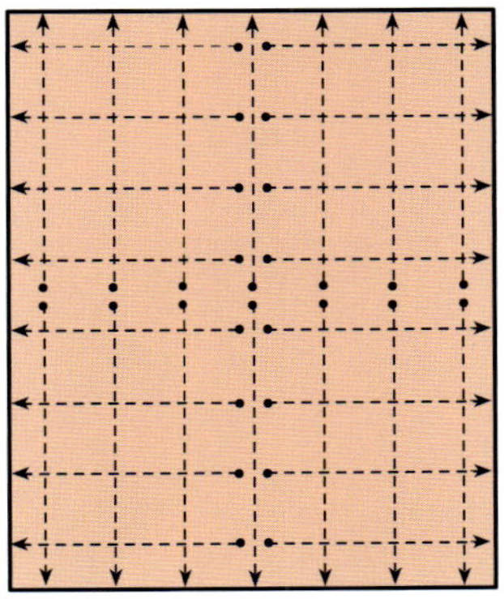

4. If machine quilting, use 1" rustproof safety pins to "pin-baste" all layers together, spacing pins approximately 4" apart. Begin at center and work toward outer edges to secure all layers. If possible, place pins away from areas that will be quilted, although pins may be removed as needed when quilting.

HAND QUILTING

The quilting stitch is a basic running stitch that forms a broken line on quilt top and backing. Stitches on quilt top and backing should be straight and equal in length.

1. Secure center of quilt in hoop or frame. Check quilt top and backing to make sure they are smooth. To help prevent puckers, always begin quilting in the center of quilt and work toward outside edges.
2. Thread needle with 18" – 20" length of quilting thread; knot one end. Using thimble, insert needle into quilt top and batting approximately 1/2" from quilting line. Bring needle up on quilting line (**Fig. 14**); when knot catches on quilt top, give thread a quick, short pull to "pop" knot through fabric into batting (**Fig. 15**).

Fig. 14

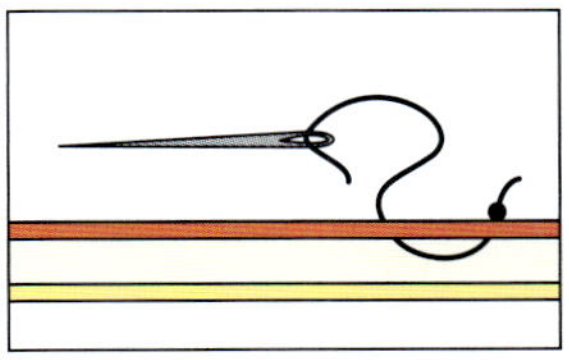

Fig. 15

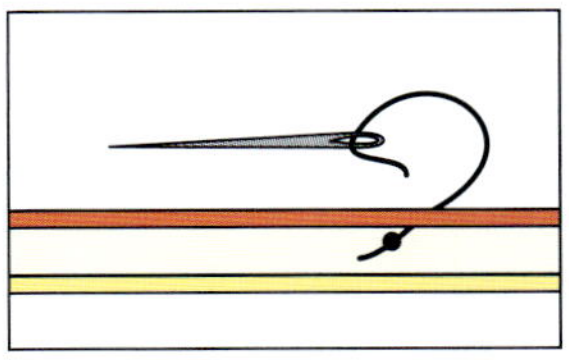

3. Holding needle with sewing hand and placing other hand underneath quilt, use thimble to push tip of needle down through all layers. As soon as needle touches finger underneath, use that finger to push tip of needle only back up through layers to top of quilt. (The amount of needle showing above fabric determines length of quilting stitch.) Referring to **Fig. 16**, rock needle up and down, taking three to six stitches before bringing needle and thread completely through layers. Check back of quilt to make sure stitches are going through all layers. If necessary, make one stitch at a time when quilting through seam allowances or along curves and corners.

Fig. 16

4. At end of thread, knot thread close to fabric and "pop" knot into batting; clip thread close to fabric.
5. Move hoop as often as necessary. Thread may be left dangling and picked up again after returning to that part of quilt.

MACHINE QUILTING METHODS

Use general-purpose thread in bobbin. Do not use quilting thread. Thread the needle of machine with general-purpose thread or transparent monofilament thread to make quilting blend with quilt top fabrics. Use decorative thread, such as a metallic or contrasting-color general-purpose thread, to make quilting lines stand out more.

Straight-Line Quilting

The term "straight-line" is somewhat deceptive, since curves (especially gentle ones) as well as straight lines can be stitched with this technique.

1. Set stitch length for six to ten stitches per inch and attach walking foot to sewing machine.
2. Determine which section of quilt will have longest continuous quilting line, oftentimes the area from center top to center bottom. Roll up and secure each edge of quilt to help reduce the bulk, keeping fabrics smooth. Smaller projects may not need to be rolled.
3. Begin stitching on longest quilting line, using very short stitches for the first $^{1}/_{4}$" to "lock" quilting. Stitch across project, using one hand on each side of walking foot to slightly spread fabric and to guide fabric through machine. Lock stitches at end of quilting line.
4. Continue machine quilting, stitching longer quilting lines first to stabilize quilt before moving on to other areas.

Free-Motion Quilting

Free-motion quilting may be free-form or may follow a marked pattern.

1. Attach darning foot to sewing machine and lower or cover feed dogs.
2. Position quilt under darning foot; lower foot. Holding top thread, take a stitch and pull bobbin thread to top of quilt. To "lock" beginning of quilting line, hold top and bobbin threads while making three to five stitches in place.
3. Use one hand on each side of darning foot to slightly spread fabric and to move fabric through the machine. Even stitch length is achieved by using smooth, flowing hand motion and steady machine speed. Slow machine speed and fast hand movement will create long stitches. Fast machine speed and slow hand movement will create short stitches. Move quilt sideways, back and forth, in a circular motion, or in a random motion to create desired designs; do not rotate quilt. Lock stitches at end of each quilting line.

BINDING

Binding encloses the raw edges of quilt. Because of its stretchiness, bias binding works well for binding projects with curves or rounded corners and tends to lie smooth and flat in any given circumstance. Binding may also be cut from straight lengthwise or crosswise grain of fabric.

MAKING CONTINUOUS BIAS STRIP BINDING

Bias strips for binding can simply be cut and pieced to desired length. However, when a long length of binding is needed, the "continuous" method is quick and accurate.

1. Cut square from binding fabric the size indicated in project instructions. Cut square in half diagonally to make two triangles.
2. With right sides together and using $^{1}/_{4}$" seam allowance, sew triangles together (**Fig. 17**); press seam allowances open.

Fig. 17

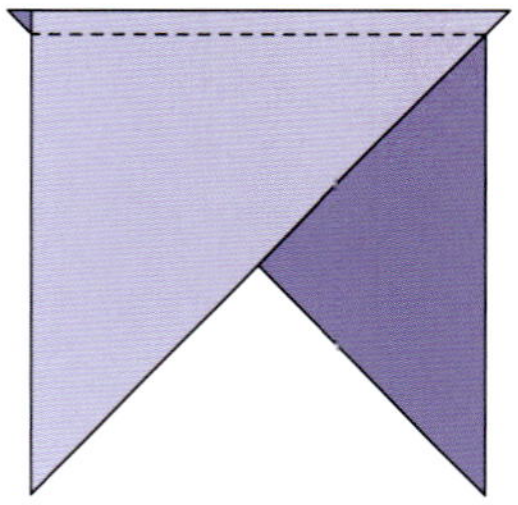

3. On wrong side of fabric, draw lines the width of binding as specified in project instructions (**Fig. 18**). Cut off any remaining fabric less than this width.

Fig. 18

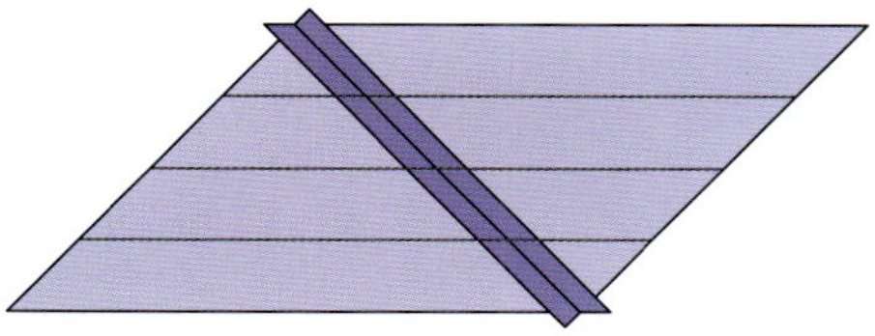

4. With right sides inside, bring short edges together to form tube; match raw edges so that first drawn line of top section meets second drawn line of bottom section (**Fig. 19**).

Fig. 19

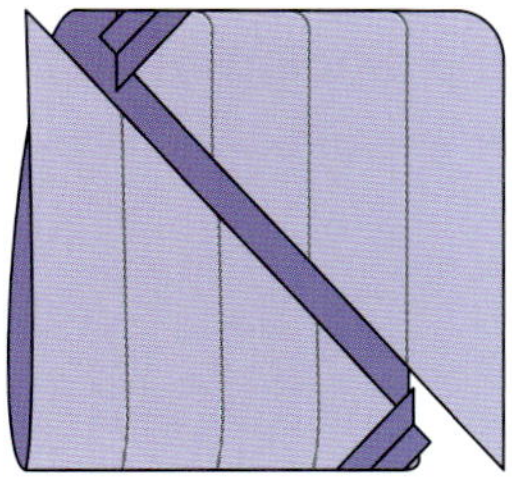

5. Carefully pin edges together by inserting pins through drawn lines at point where drawn lines intersect, making sure pins go through intersections on both sides. Using 1/4" seam allowance, sew edges together; press seam allowances open.

6. To cut continuous strip, begin cutting along first drawn line (**Fig. 20**). Continue cutting along drawn line around tube.

Fig. 20

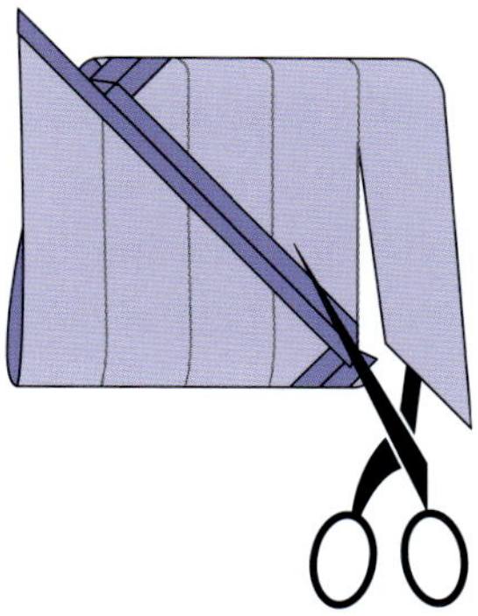

7. Trim ends of bias strip square.

8. Matching wrong sides and raw edges, carefully press bias strip in half lengthwise to complete binding.

ATTACHING BINDING WITH MITERED CORNERS

1. Beginning with one end near center on bottom edge of quilt, lay binding around quilt to make sure that seams in binding will not end up at a corner. Adjust placement if necessary. Matching raw edges of binding to raw edge of quilt top, pin binding to right side of quilt along one edge.

2. When you reach first corner, mark 1/4" from corner of quilt top (**Fig. 21**).

Fig. 21

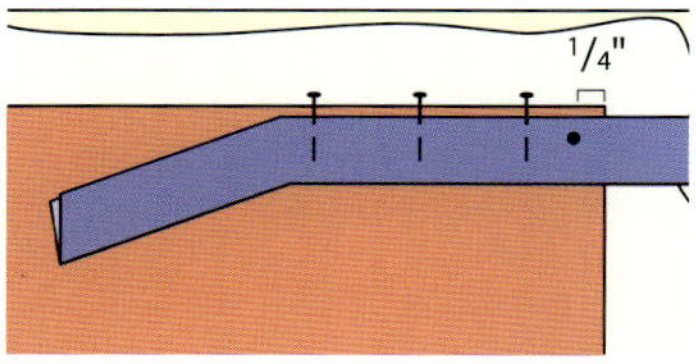

3. Beginning approximately 10" from end of binding and using 1/4" seam allowance, sew binding to quilt, backstitching at beginning of stitching and at mark (**Fig. 22**). Lift needle out of fabric and clip thread.

Fig. 22

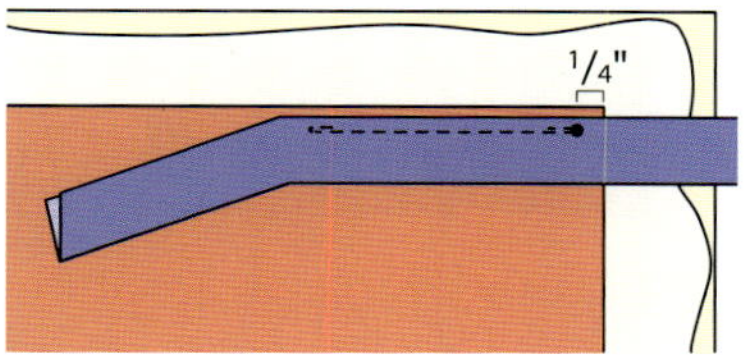

4. Fold binding as shown in **Figs. 23 – 24** and pin binding to adjacent side, matching raw edges. When you've reached the next corner, mark 1/4" from edge of quilt top.

Fig. 23

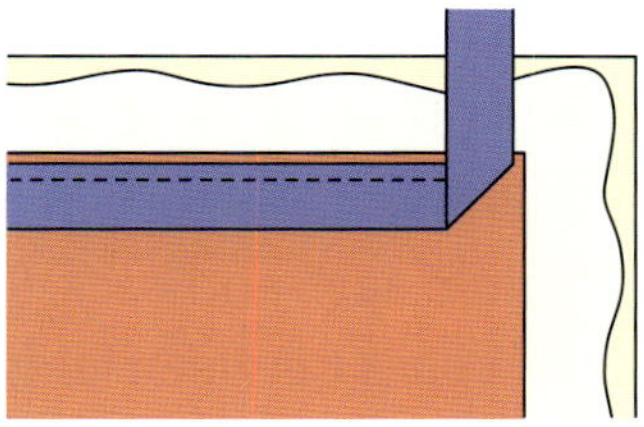

Fig. 24

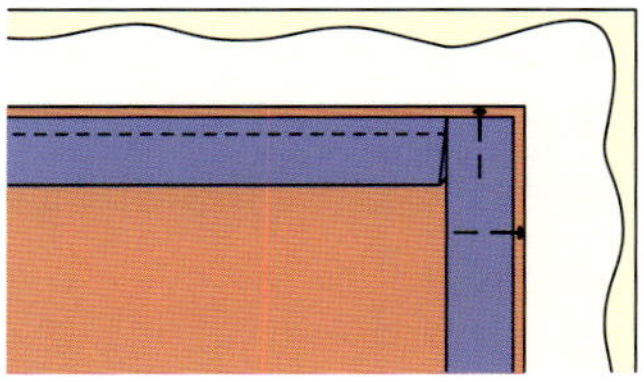

5. Backstitching at edge of quilt top, sew pinned binding to quilt (**Fig. 25**); backstitch at the next mark. Lift needle out of fabric and clip thread.

Fig. 25

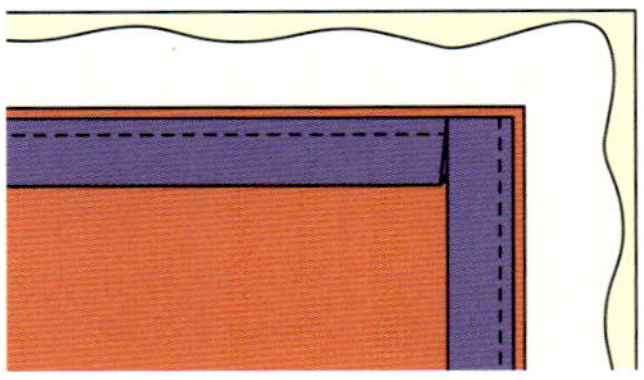

6. Continue sewing binding to quilt, stopping approximately 10" from starting point (**Fig. 26**).

Fig. 26

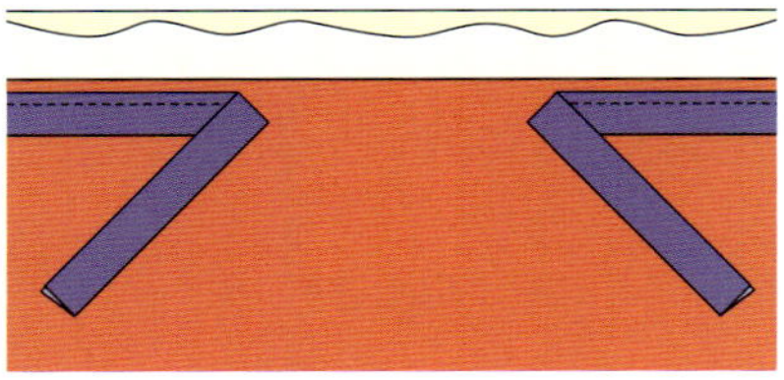

7. Bring beginning and end of binding to center of opening and fold each end back, leaving a $^1/_4$" space between folds (**Fig. 27**). Finger press folds.

Fig. 27

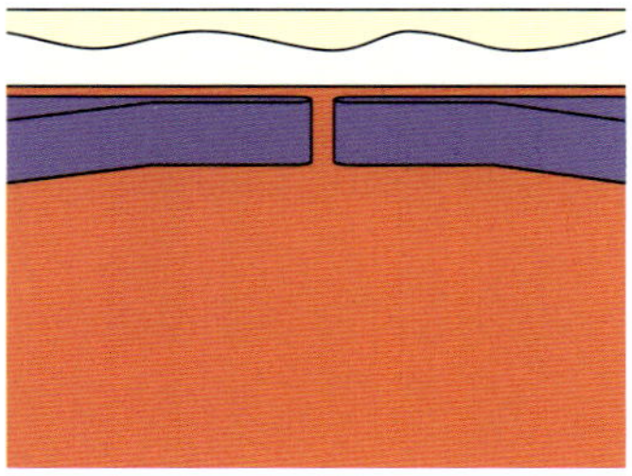

8. Unfold ends of binding and draw a line across wrong side in finger-pressed crease. Draw a line through the lengthwise pressed fold of binding at the same spot to create a cross mark. With edge of ruler at cross mark, line up 45° angle marking on ruler with one long side of binding. Draw a diagonal line from edge to edge. Repeat on remaining end, making sure that the two diagonal lines are angled the same way **(Fig. 28)**.

Fig. 28

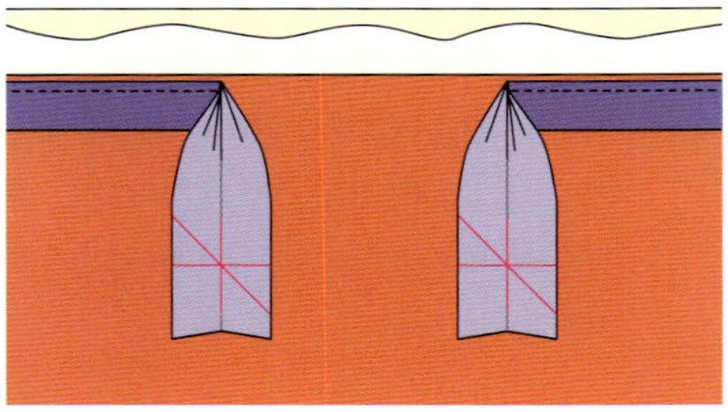

9. Matching right sides and diagonal lines, pin binding ends together at right angles (**Fig. 29**).

Fig. 29

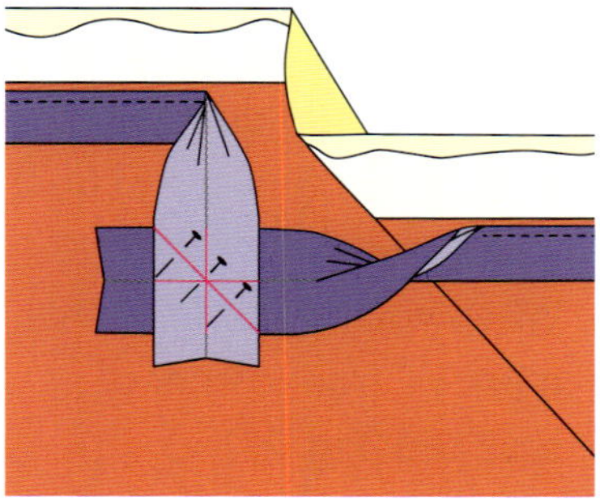

10. Machine stitch along diagonal line (**Fig. 30**), removing pins as you stitch.

Fig. 30

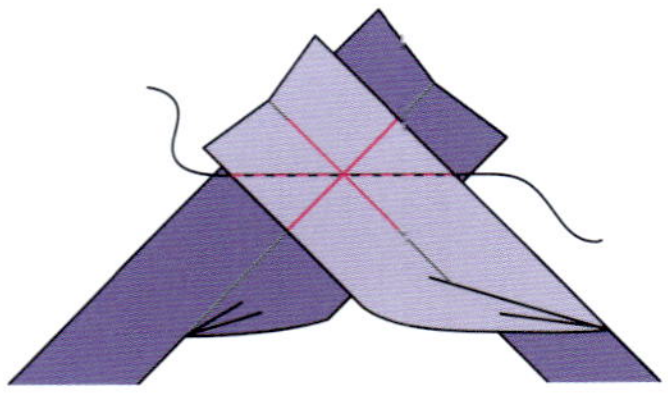

11. Lay binding against quilt to double check that it is correct length.
12. Trim binding ends, leaving $^1/_4$" seam allowance; press seam open. Stitch binding to quilt.
13. Trim backing and batting a scant $^1/_4$" larger than quilt top so that batting and backing will fill the binding when it is folded over to quilt backing.

14. On one edge of quilt, fold binding over to quilt backing and pin pressed edge in place, covering stitching line (**Fig. 31**). On adjacent side, fold binding over, forming a mitered corner (**Fig. 32**). Repeat to pin remainder of binding in place.

Fig. 31

Fig. 32

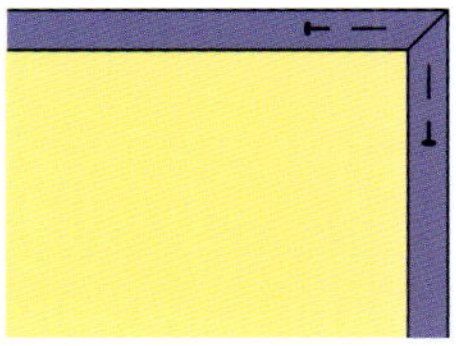

15. Blindstitch binding to backing, taking care not to stitch through to front of quilt. To blindstitch, come up at 1, go down at 2, and come up at 3 (**Fig. 33**). Length of stitches may be varied as desired.

Fig. 33

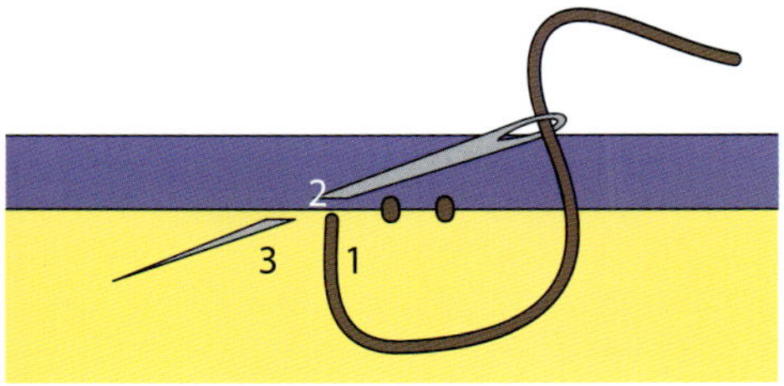

ATTACHING BINDING WITH OVERLAPPED CORNERS

1. Matching raw edges and using 1/4" seam allowance, sew a length of binding to top and bottom edges on right side of quilt.
2. Trim backing and batting from top and bottom edges a scant 1/4" larger than quilt top so that batting and backing will fill the binding when it is folded over to quilt backing.
3. Trim ends of top and bottom binding even with edges of quilt top. Fold binding over to quilt backing and pin pressed edges in place, covering stitching line (**Fig. 34**); blindstitch binding to backing.

Fig. 34

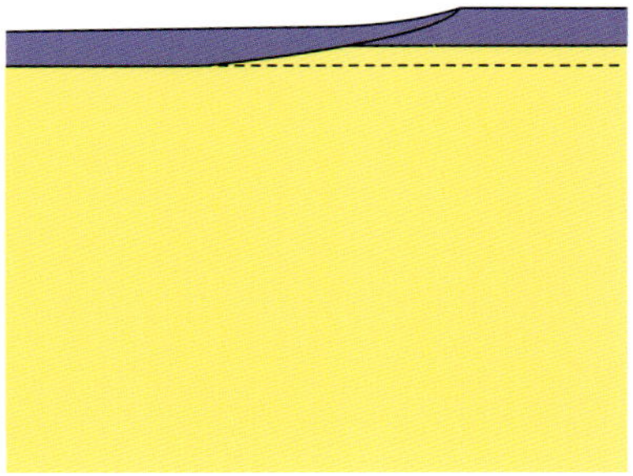

4. Leaving approximately 1 1/2" of binding at each end, stitch a length of binding to each side edge of quilt. Trim backing and batting as in Step 2.
5. Trim each end of binding 1/2" longer than bound edge. Fold each end of binding over to quilt backing (**Fig. 35**); pin in place. Fold binding over to quilt backing and blindstitch in place, taking care not to stitch through to front of quilt.

Fig. 35

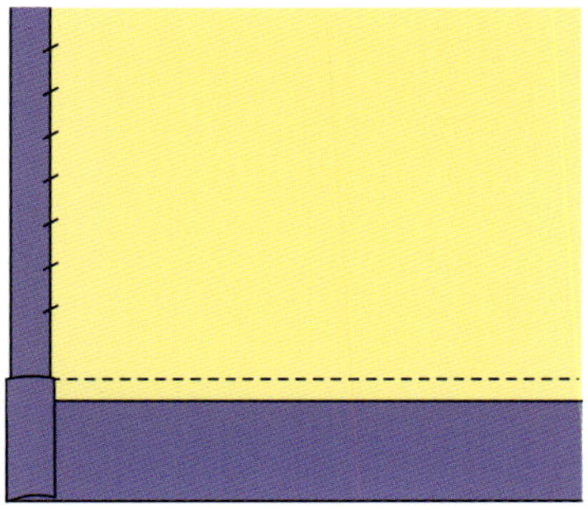

SIGNING AND DATING YOUR QUILT

A completed quilt is a work of art and should be signed and dated. There are many different ways to do this and numerous books on the subject. The label should reflect the style of the quilt, the occasion or person for which it was made, and the quilter's own particular talents. Following are suggestions for recording the history of quilt or adding a sentiment for future generations.

- Embroider quilter's name, date, and any additional information on quilt top or backing. Matching floss, such as cream floss on white border, will leave a subtle record. Bright or contrasting floss will make the information stand out.
- Make label from muslin and use permanent marker to write information. Use different colored permanent markers to make label more decorative. Stitch label to back of quilt.
- Use photo-transfer paper to add image to white or cream fabric label. Stitch label to back of quilt.
- Piece an extra block from quilt top pattern to use as label. Add information with permanent fabric pen. Appliqué block to back of quilt.

Metric Conversion Chart

Inches x 2.54 = centimeters (cm)	Yards x .9144 = meters (m)
Inches x 25.4 = millimeters (mm)	Yards x 91.44 = centimeters (cm)
Inches x .0254 = meters (m)	Centimeters x .3937 = inches (")
	Meters x 1.0936 = yards (yd)

Standard Equivalents

1/8"	3.2 mm	0.32 cm	1/8 yard	11.43 cm	0.11 m
1/4"	6.35 mm	0.635 cm	1/4 yard	22.86 cm	0.23 m
3/8"	9.5 mm	0.95 cm	3/8 yard	34.29 cm	0.34 m
1/2"	12.7 mm	1.27 cm	1/2 yard	45.72 cm	0.46 m
5/8"	15.9 mm	1.59 cm	5/8 yard	57.15 cm	0.57 m
3/4"	19.1 mm	1.91 cm	3/4 yard	68.58 cm	0.69 m
7/8"	22.2 mm	2.22 cm	7/8 yard	80 cm	0.8 m
1 "	25.4 mm	2.54 cm	1 yard	91.44 cm	0.91 m